"My personal struggle against the forces o[f] days as a believer but intensified as I served o[n] not want to let go of those we came to reach for Christ. Then, hundreds of missionaries told us that spiritual warfare was the one area they felt least prepared to face. Now I am working with American seminary students, and many confess they have little preparation for facing personal attacks by that same enemy. *Victory over the Enemy* is an excellent resource for understanding this spiritual struggle and how we can live victoriously in Christ!"

— **Don Dent**, professor of missions, Gateway Seminary

"Having read numerous book endorsements over the years, I have a certain distaste for the timeworn statement, 'If you can read only one book about [name the subject], this is the one you should choose.' Still, I am convinced that *Victory over the Enemy* is just such a book. Scriptural, practical, and desperately needed, this is the primer you should read alongside your Bible. You'll never again see the world, the flesh, and the devil through the same eyes. And, by God's grace you will begin walking in victory."

— **Tom Elliff**, president emeritus, International Mission Board

"*Victory over the Enemy* reminds Christians that we are in a daily battle against this world, our flesh, and Satan. This book gives the reader the tools to both understand and recognize our enemy as well as stand against him. But the gem of this book is its faithfulness to the Scriptures and the emphasis on our union with Christ, the indwelling presence and power of the Holy Spirit, and our growth toward Christlikeness. It is my personal hope that this book will propel readers to have a new or renewed longing for the Word of God."

— **Lesley Hildreth**, women's discipleship director of
The Summit Church, Durham, North Carolina

"Chuck Lawless and Bill Cook have written an incredible study and a valuable tool that will help believers understand how God equips and empowers us to overcome the enemy. This practical book is rich in biblical content and thorough in explanation, and it teaches us how the enemy attacks, how God provides for his people, and how we, in God's power, fight the enemy on a daily basis."

—**Jaye Martin**, Jaye Martin Ministries

"Drs. Chuck Lawless and Bill Cook have done the church a great service. Lawless and Cook equip us to face the battle against the world, the flesh, and the devil because our Lord has already won the victory. So, read alongside others and invite them to fight sin and Satan with God's Word, by faith, and in reliance on the Holy Spirit."

—**Juan R. Sanchez**, senior pastor,
High Pointe Baptist Church, Austin, Texas

"We are in a spiritual war, and we are in trouble, not because the enemy is so powerful, but because we either ignore or have never heard that God has provided the means for us to fight and win. Building on their previous work, Bill Cook and Chuck Lawless have written the most accessible, practical guide I have seen on spiritual warfare. It explains what God has done and what we can (and should) do to walk in victory. Far from wasting time on speculation, *Victory over the Enemy* repeatedly points the reader to Scripture and the One who is already victorious!"

—**Stuart Sheehan**, president and CEO,
World Hope Bible Institute

"In *Victory over the Enemy*, Chuck Lawless and Bill Cook bring the truth about spiritual warfare to the level of laity without dumbing down its profundity. They expertly guide readers to face the enemy and be victorious even in this day of increasing biblical illiteracy and textual tone deafness. This volume is not a luxury for the Christian—it is a necessity!"

—**Robert Smith Jr.**, Charles T. Carter Baptist
Chair of Divinity, Beeson Divinity School

VICTORY
over the
ENEMY

WILLIAM F. COOK III
& CHUCK LAWLESS

VICTORY
over the
ENEMY

*Defeating the World,
the Flesh, and the Devil*

ACADEMIC
BRENTWOOD, TENNESSEE

From Bill

I want to dedicate this book to the Ninth and O Baptist Church for the privilege of being your pastor since 2001. Your kindness, love, encouragement, and support to me and my family mean more than I could ever express in words. Thank you! #naobc4life

From Chuck

I dedicate this book to the members of the two Ohio churches I served as pastor: Mt. Calvary Baptist Church in Harrison and Rolling Hills Baptist Church in Fairfield. I cannot fully understand why you called me as a young pastor, tolerated my leadership mistakes, and prayerfully supported me as your under-shepherd. I pray your willingness to take a risk on me many years ago has produced fruit.

From Bill and Chuck

Both of us know we could not do what we do were it not for God's grace. In grace, he has given us our spouses whose support and prayers drive us forward. Jaylynn and Pam, we dedicate this book to you.

Contents

Part 3: Disciplining Our Lives for Victory

Foreword

Spiritual warfare may be one of the most misunderstood issues that emerges from a reading of the Bible. The bizarre and wildly fanciful things I have heard over the years made me wonder if the person I was reading or listening to had actually read the Bible. And make no mistakes about it: the stakes are extremely high when this occurs.

Any teaching that is detached from Holy Scripture will run the risk of distortion and even heresy. This is especially true when it comes to spiritual warfare. The ever-present danger of stepping and sinking into deadly spiritual quicksand demands that we pursue a better and wiser path in formulating our understanding of spiritual realities. Being tethered to the inerrant and all-sufficient Word of God is crucial if we are to keep our souls from serious spiritual damage. Our understanding of the doctrine of spiritual warfare, or any doctrine for that matter, must be grounded in the Word of God.

This bedrock conviction is why I am delighted to commend *Victory over the Enemy* by my dear friends, Bill Cook and Chuck

Lawless. Both are superb scholars as well as seasoned pastors. They have spent time in the war room and served on the battle-field. They are dedicated to our war manual, the Bible, and they know who our commander-in-chief is: King Jesus.

This book has many strengths, but I highlight two. First, it is biblical and theologically faithful. There are no wild speculations in this book, only that which is true and faithful to Scripture. They show us what the Bible says and teaches about spiritual warfare. Period! Second, it is filled with practical wisdom and instruction for engaging the evil one (the devil and his demons). It guides us to build into our lives biblical disciplines and practices that ensure we experience the victory that is already ours through the death, burial, and resurrection of the captain of our salvation, the Lord Jesus Christ.

This is a book that will serve well the body of Christ for years, even decades, to come. Spiritual warfare is real. It is not some mythical fairy tale from a worldview that is no longer tenable. We must be prepared to engage the battle, and this book will equip you to do just that.

Daniel L. Akin
President, Southeastern Baptist Theological Seminary

INTRODUCTION

Where Are We Headed?

Victory over the Enemy is intended as a sequel to our earlier work, *Spiritual Warfare in the Storyline of Scripture.*[1] While the two volumes overlap at points, this book stands as an independent work intended for a wider audience. We wrote the first volume to alert the church to the danger of underestimating the significant amount of biblical material on Satan and demons. At the same time, we offered believers help to battle God's archenemy, the devil.

This volume differs in several ways from our earlier work. First, the discussion here includes a broader examination of the Christian's enemy: the world, the flesh (indwelling sin), and the devil. While our first volume was often descriptive of our enemy's tactics, this work is more prescriptive by delineating the believer's resources in the battle and strategies for fighting the

---

[1] William F. Cook and Chuck Lawless, *Spiritual Warfare in the Storyline of Scripture* (Nashville: B&H Academic, 2019).

enemy. The Christian life is a daily battle for holiness against the three-headed monster of the world, the flesh, and the devil. While this depiction of our enemy sounds ominous, Christians must never forget, "the one who is in you is greater than the one who is in the world" (1 John 4:4).

A second difference between this volume and our earlier one is that this work focuses attention on the believer's sanctification. While justification happens at the moment of conversion, sanctification is a lifelong process whereby Christians are conformed more and more into the image of Christ (Rom 8:29). Sanctification takes place as Christians battle the world, the flesh, and the devil. The better we know our enemy and understand their tactics, the more equipped we will be to recognize them at work and stand against them.

A third difference between the two volumes is a greater emphasis on the spiritual resources God provides his children so they do not love the world, do put indwelling sin to death, and do resist the devil. For example, I (Bill) focus attention on the believer's union with Christ and the indwelling presence and power of the Holy Spirit. Chuck will help you understand the importance of spiritual disciplines like reading and memorizing the Word of God and fasting to grow into Christlikeness. These are just a couple of examples we explore in the following pages.

The good news is that God has not left us to fight these battles in our own strength. Peter put it this way, "His divine power has given us everything required for life and godliness through the knowledge of him who called us by his own glory and goodness. By these he has given us very great and precious promises, so that through them you may share in the divine nature, escaping the corruption that is in the world because of evil desire" (2 Pet 1:3–4).

The book unfolds in three parts. The first part focuses attention on our enemy—the world, the flesh, and the devil. The second part highlights God's provisions for overcoming the enemy. The final part details key strategies for living in victory over that enemy. Our goal is that you recognize the enemy, turn your attention even more significantly to God's grace and protection, and then build some practical disciplines in your life for victory.

You will likely recognize some overlap in the chapters and the parts. For example, the topic of prayer will echo throughout this book. It will also be difficult to read this book without seeing the importance of the church in this battle. In addition, you will hear often about the significance of the Word of God as one part of the armor. We focus a great deal of attention on important passages of Scripture, and we do that unashamedly because all God intends us to know to live in victory over the enemy is revealed in the Word.

All this repetition is intentional, as we want to emphasize what God has given us for the victory. Thus, pause and consider deeply these teachings when you hear them stated more than once. Don't skim the content, even if you've read it previously in this book.

We are deeply concerned with the evident lack of passion for personal holiness in much of the church today. On a regular basis, social media announces the fall of supposed evangelical "superstars." However, what has been true in some pulpits (or sitting at high tables) has been equally true among the pews (or theater seats). Worship services are trending more and more toward concert-style entertainment. Atmosphere trumps substance. Many in the pews are clamoring for more and more sermons focused on "felt needs" and less expository preaching with substantive biblical content. Christian marriages are dissolving at an alarming rate, and the sexual revolution is affecting many congregations. Church leadership practices look more like corporate models than biblical models.

Behind all of this is an evident lack of passion and zeal for the glory of God. Some of this is the result of the insidious work of the devil, using the world to appeal to the inward sinful inclinations of those sitting in the pews and standing behind the pulpits. In fact, separating the roles played by the world, the flesh, and the devil is not an easy task. The Bible focuses on each of these three in different contexts. Only occasionally are the three found together as in Eph 2:1–3, "And you were dead in your trespasses and sins in which you previously walked according to the ways of this world, according to the ruler of the power of the air, the spirit now working in the disobedient. We too all previously lived among them in our fleshly desires, carrying out the inclinations of our flesh and thoughts, and we were by nature children under wrath as the others were also." We face these three enemies, but we do so wearing the full armor of God.

The reality of the battles the church faces today may be discouraging, but we are encouraged by what God is doing throughout the world. God is building an army of young people committed to holy living who have an evangelistic zeal evident in their desire to take the gospel to the nations. Chuck and I have had the privilege of working with this generation as we have served on the faculties of Southern Baptist seminaries. At the same time, we have a passion for God to be glorified in the local church. We are both pastors at heart. I have served for more than twenty years as the lead pastor at the Ninth and O Baptist Church in Louisville. Chuck has both significant pastoral and missions experience. As we move into the final seasons of our ministries, our burden for the church increases.

We desire for God's people to grow in their passion and love for Jesus and in their desire to take the gospel across the street and around the world. We pray that this work will assist you to live for God's glory by the indwelling power of the Holy Spirit. *Soli Deo Gloria!*

PART 1

Recognizing Our Enemy: The World, the Flesh, and the Devil

CHAPTER 1

Resist the Devil

M any contemporary people speak of the devil in the same breath as ghouls, goblins, and the "fantastic beasts" of Harry Potter. The modern naturalistic worldview permeating Western civilization has no place for the supernatural. Still others are captivated by an unhealthy fascination with the reality of an unseen world of spiritual beings (angels and demons). C. S. Lewis, in the preface to his classic work *The Screwtape Letters*, warns about the danger of both extremes, "There are two equal and opposite errors into which our race can fall about the devils. One is to disbelieve in their existence. The other is to believe, and to feel an excessive and unhealthy interest in them. They themselves [the devils] are equally pleased by both errors and hail a materialist or a magician with the same delight."[1]

---

[1] C. S. Lewis, *The Screwtape Letters with Screwtape Proposes a Toast*, Signature Classics (New York: HarperOne, 2001), ix.

To deny the reality of the devil is not an option for evangelical Christians. The Bible is the authoritative source for understanding life. In the Bible, Satan is God's archenemy. Clinton Arnold describes the devil as "an intelligent, powerful spirit-being that is thoroughly evil and is directly involved in perpetuating evil in the lives of individuals as well as on a much larger scale."[2] John Stott put the matter this way:

> We need to rid our minds of the medieval caricature of Satan. Dispensing with the horns, the hooves and the tail, we are left with a diabolical portrait of a spiritual being, highly intelligent, immensely powerful and utterly unscrupulous. Jesus himself both believed in his existence and warned us of his power. He called him "the prince of this world," much as Paul called him "the ruler of the kingdom of the air." He has therefore a throne and a kingdom, and under his command is an army of malignant spirits who are described in Scripture as "the powers of this dark world," and "the spiritual forces of evil in the heavenly realms" (John 12:31; Eph 6:12).[3]

As ominous as this sounds, Satan is *not* God's equal. He was created by God, exists under God's sovereign control, is limited by God in what God allows him to do, was decisively defeated at the cross, and one day will be thrown into the lake of fire (Col 2:15; Rev 20:10). Until that day, believers are called to "resist the devil" (Jas 4:7).

---

[2] Clinton E. Arnold, *3 Crucial Questions about Spiritual Warfare* (Grand Rapids: Baker, 1997), 35.

[3] John R. W. Stott, *What Christ Thinks of the Church* (Wheaton, IL: Harold Shaw, 1990), 50.

Satan in the Bible: An Overview

Although our ancient foe slithers into the storyline of Scripture in the beginning (Gen 3:1; cf. Rev 12:9), explicit references accrue in an exponential fashion—beginning slowly in the Old Testament and increasing substantially in the New Testament.

Satan in the Old Testament

Satan is explicitly mentioned in only three passages in the OT (Job 1–2; Zechariah 3; 1 Chr 21:1), but his role in Scripture is apparent from the beginning. From Genesis 3 onward, Satan constantly opposes God and seeks to destroy humanity. Yet, as already mentioned, the way the biblical authors describe Satan *always* makes clear that he is inferior to God. But what are we to make of Satan's origin and fall?

Genesis 1:31 reads, "God saw all that he had made, and it was very good indeed." Therefore, even the angelic world was created good. At some point between Gen 1:31 and Gen 3:1, however, Satan and his demons must have rebelled against God. As to when this rebellion took place, the Bible does not tell us—and speculation on the matter is not helpful.

The Bible, however, does offer some hints on the nature of Satan's fall. For example, Jesus said in John 8:44, "You are of your father the devil, and you want to carry out your father's desires. He was a murderer from the beginning and does not stand in the truth, because there is no truth in him. When he tells a lie, he speaks from his own nature, because he is a liar and the father of lies." While Jesus is confronting the religious leaders in this passage, Jesus's comments provide insight into the devil's *fall* from the truth.

Another New Testament passage that points to Satan's fall is 1 Tim 3:6. Paul wrote, "He must not be a new convert, or he might become conceited and incur the same condemnation as the devil." Paul was warning Timothy about the danger of appointing a new convert to the role of an elder. We should likely understand from Paul's comment that Satan suffered condemnation for the sin of pride, the same sin a young convert appointed to the position of elder is in danger of committing.

If this thinking is correct, there are two passages in the Old Testament that may allude to the devil's fall into the sin of pride: Isa 14:3–23 and Ezek 28:2–19. There is significant debate over whether the two passages refer only to two earthly monarchs, or if the exaggerated language may also point back to Satan's fall. A definitive answer may not be possible. However, Christopher Wright offers a mediating position on these two Old Testament texts:

> [It is] a dubious exercise to build doctrinal statements about the devil or the "underworld" upon them [Isa 14:4–21 and Ezek 28:1–17]. Nevertheless, we may discern the fingerprints of Satan in what is described in these poems, since it is clear that these arrogant human beings [the kings of Babylon and Tyre, respectively] were brought low because of their blasphemous pride and boasting against God. Indeed, they are portrayed as usurping God's throne. In the poem, such claims are probably metaphorical for the human being's *hybris*, but they have a spiritual counterpart that is recognizably satanic.[4]

---

[4] Christopher J. H. Wright, *The God I Don't Understand: Reflections on Tough Questions of Faith* (Grand Rapids: Zondervan, 2008), 40. I am

Based on these passages, Satan's fall may have been the result of pride that convinced him of the lie that he could unseat God as Sovereign Lord. Satan could not have been any more wrong.

Satan carries out much of his wickedness through demons (Mark 3:22). Demons are supernatural spirit-beings who were created by God, fell away from God, and work under the authority of Satan. Demons are not mentioned many times in the Old Testament. When demons are mentioned, they are associated with pagan gods and idolatrous worship (Deut 32:17; Ps 106:37). Just as God can use Satan in the accomplishment of his purposes, so the same is true with demonic spirits (1 Kgs 22:19–23).

One should not immediately think that the influence of Satan and demons removes personal responsibility for our sinful actions. For example, although Satan was involved in the sin of Adam and Eve in the garden, God punished *them* for their sinful choices (Gen 3:16–19; cf. Judg 9; 1 Kgs 22; 2 Chr 18).[5] The same was true of David. Although Satan incited him to take a military census (1 Chr 21), this satanic involvement did not excuse David of his sin against God.

The stories of Job and Daniel also reveal that people are not privy to what is transpiring in the unseen world of spiritual reality. Nowhere did Job appear to understand that the terrible tragedies he endured were the result of Satanic attacks due to

---

indebted for the reference to Graham A. Cole, *Against the Darkness: The Doctrine of Angels, Satan, and Demons* (Wheaton, IL: Crossway, 2019), 93.

[5] Moses reported God's curses in reverse order from humanity's blame-shifting: Adam blamed Eve (3:12), Eve blamed the serpent (3:13); then God cursed the serpent (3:14–15), Eve (3:16), and finally Adam (3:17). Overall, this suggests that although the serpent is cursed, God began and ended with Adam, thus highlighting his importance as head not only of his family but also of humanity.

his godliness (Job 1–2). Nor did Daniel appear to have any idea that a delay in answering his prayer was the result of a spiritual conflict in the heavenlies (Dan 10). Eventually, Daniel was given insight into what was taking place and the intervention of the angel Michael. This pulling back of the curtain that allowed Daniel to gain insight into the activity of the spiritual realm is very rare in Scripture.

In summary, two facts are quite clear from this brief OT survey: (1) we are responsible for our sin even in the case of satanic/demonic involvement, and (2) apart from divine revelation *in Scripture*, what transpires in the unseen spiritual realm will remain a mystery.

Satan in the New Testament

The New Testament teaching on Satan and demons represents a substantial increase from the Old Testament. Indeed, Jesus's ministry begins with a confrontation with Satan in the wilderness (Matt 4:1–11; Mark 1:13–14; Luke 4:1–13). Furthermore, Jesus's ministry in the Synoptic Gospels is characterized by powerful exorcisms (Mark 1:21–28; 5:1–20; 7:24–30; 9:14–29).[6]

The New Testament does not underestimate Satan's substantial power. Jesus referred to him as "the ruler of this world" (John 12:31; 14:30; 16:11). Paul referred to Satan as "the god of this age" (2 Cor 4:4). John underlined the scope of Satan's authority: "The whole world is under the sway of the evil one" (1 John 5:19). The author of Hebrews added that the devil is

---

[6] For a more comprehensive examination of these passages, see Cook and Lawless, *Spiritual Warfare in the Storyline of Scripture*, 50–62 (see intro., n. 1).

"the one holding the power of death" (Heb 2:14). Yet—to be clear—the New Testament often uses statements like these to highlight the supremacy of Christ, who "cast [Satan] out" at the cross (John 12:31–32), illumines hearts that Satan tries in vain to blind (2 Cor 4:6), "destroys the devil's works" (1 John 3:8), and took on a human nature so that "through his death he might destroy . . . the devil" (Heb 2:14).

Satanic opposition to Jesus continues after Christ's ascension in the book of Acts, where the devil attempted to hinder the advancement of the gospel into the Greco-Roman world (Acts 5:1–16; 8:5–25; 13:6–12; 16:16–18; 19:11–20).[7] Yet how does Acts end? Luke ends Acts with a summary statement about Paul's ministry: "[He was] proclaiming the kingdom of God and teaching about the Lord Jesus Christ with all boldness and *without hindrance*" (28:31, italics added).

The epistolary literature and Revelation highlight many of the ways the devil attempts to derail the people of God. The following list is a sample of Satan's methods to destroy the church and hinder the sanctification of God's people:

- persecuting the church (Rev 12:15–17)
- promoting false teachers and heretical doctrine (2 Cor 11:3–4, 12–15; Col 2:20–21; 1 Tim 4:1–2; 2 Tim 2:24–26; Rev 2:24)
- setting traps for church leaders: pride, promiscuity, greed (1 Tim 3:6–7)
- encouraging moral compromise within the church (Acts 5:1–11)

---

[7] For further discussion of such occurrences in Acts, see Cook and Lawless, *Spiritual Warfare in the Storyline of Scripture*, 81–97.

- exploiting sinful tendencies of individual believers (Eph 4:26–27)
- tempting with false wisdom (1 Cor 2:6–8; Jas 3:14–16)
- propagating idolatrous worship (1 Cor 10:18–22)
- seeking to cause churches to do the right thing in the wrong way (2 Cor 2:10–11)
- tempting believers to do God's work in the power of the flesh rather than the power of the Spirit (2 Cor 10:3–5)
- tempting believers to turn from God during times of intense suffering (1 Tim 5:14–15; cf. Job 1–2)

In light of Satan's arsenal of schemes and tactics, we must heed James's exhortation: "Submit to God. Resist the devil, and he will flee from you. Draw near to God, and he will draw near to you" (Jas 4:7–8). Doug Moo insightfully observes that "the commands [*resist* the devil / *draw* near to God] . . . unpack the significance of 'submitting' to God. Placing ourselves under God's authority means, negatively, that we firmly refuse to bow to the devil's authority."[8] To do this, we must recognize the devil's schemes when we see them.

Satan's Role in Biblical Turning Points

This is a conscious battle, one that appears at the key junctures in redemptive history: creation/fall, redemption, and consummation. In this section, we will take a closer look at each of these turning points.

---

[8] Douglas J. Moo, *The Letter of James*, Pillar New Testament Commentary (Grand Rapids: Eerdmans, 2000), 193.

Creation and the Fall: The War Begins

The battle of the ages began in the garden of Eden.[9] Genesis 2 concludes by highlighting Adam and Eve's innocence (v. 25). In the opening of chapter 3, the narrator contrasts Adam and Eve's innocence with the serpent's cunning nature (3:1). The narrator next describes Adam and Eve's fall into sin, their banishment from Eden, and God's promise of coming victory through the seed of the woman (3:1–19).

The serpent seemingly appeared from out of nowhere, immediately challenged God's command to the couple, and then slandered God's character (3:1, 4).[10] Adam and Eve failed to understand what was at stake in their encounter with the serpent. Eve replied immediately to the serpent's questioning of God's word (3:2). While Eve's summary of God's command corresponds in a general way to what God said earlier, the subtle differences indicate her failure to take God's word with the utmost seriousness on this matter. The following demonstrates the subtle changes Eve made to God's instruction:

---

[9] We discuss this passage with greater detail in Cook and Lawless, *Spiritual Warfare in the Storyline of Scripture*, 8–13.

[10] Why a snake? Naselli helpfully writes, "A serpent has two major strategies: deceive and devour. As a general rule, the form a serpent takes depends on its strategy. When a serpent in Scripture attempts to deceive, it's a snake [think Gen 3]. When a serpent attempts to devour, it's a dragon [think Rev 12]. Snakes deceive; dragons devour. Snakes tempt and lie; dragons attack and murder. Snakes backstab; dragons assault." Andrew David Naselli, *The Serpent and the Serpent Slayer*, Short Studies in Biblical Theology (Wheaton, IL: Crossway, 2020), 18. See also Naselli's treatment of Genesis 3 (33–47).

> Genesis 2:15–17: The Lord God took the man and placed him in the garden of Eden to work it and watch over it. And the Lord God commanded the man, "You are free to eat from any tree of the garden, but you must not eat from the tree of the knowledge of good and evil, for on the day you eat from it, you will certainly die."

> Genesis 3:2–3: The woman said to the serpent, "We may eat the fruit from the trees in the garden. But about the fruit of the tree in the middle of the garden, God said, 'You must not eat it or touch it, or you will die.'"

These subtle changes should not be pressed to mean that God requires us to quote his Word perfectly from memory to claim his promises or to wield his Word as a spiritual sword in our battle with Satan. Rather, Eve's subsequent actions revealed her failure to genuinely trust the *meaning* of God's command to them. Adam and Eve's response to the serpent's enticement revealed a longing for autonomy, indeed, a longing for divinity. Adam and Eve had forgotten already that God created them in *his* image (1:26–27).

Next, the author describes Adam and Eve's sinful acts: "When the woman *saw* that the tree was good for food, and that it was a delight to the *eyes*, and that the tree was *desirable* to make one wise, she *took* from its fruit and *ate*; and she gave also to her husband with her, and he ate" (3:6 NASB, italics added). Old Testament scholar Derek Kidner observes that the verbs "take" and "eat" describe very simple actions, but those acts required a costly response by God—the death of Jesus.[11]

---

[11] Derek Kidner, *Genesis: An Introduction and Commentary*, Tyndale Old Testament Commentaries 1 (Downers Grove, IL: InterVarsity, 1967), 68.

When God confronts Adam about his sin, Adam blames God for giving Eve to him ("The woman you gave to be with me—she gave me some fruit from the tree, and I ate," Gen 3:12). When God confronts Eve, she blames the serpent and its deception of her ("The serpent deceived me, and I ate," v. 13; cf. John 8:44). In Gen 3:14–19, the devastating consequences for their sin are delineated. God begins with the serpent and finishes with Adam. God's curse of the serpent would result in a perpetual conflict between the woman's seed and the serpent's seed. God's words appear to go beyond the serpent and refer to Satan and his demons ("offspring"). God's point is that there will be a perpetual war between satanic forces and humanity. Ultimately, "the seed of the woman" refers to Jesus Christ, who delivers the fatal blow by crushing the serpent's head (v. 15). This crushing blow to the serpent took place at the cross.

The consequences of Adam and Eve's sin are devastating (vv. 16–19). What a contrast life for them was before the fall versus after:

- Before the fall, they enjoyed a full, satisfying, and abundant life. After the fall, they suffered heartache and pain.
- Before the fall, they enjoyed God's abundant provision, and work was pleasurable. After the fall, they learned to labor for food, and that work was drudgery.
- Before the fall, they enjoyed unbroken fellowship with God and one another. After the fall, they experienced alienation, conflict, loneliness, and death.

Everything changed with the fall of Adam and Eve. They had lost their battle—but God had already set in motion his plan to bring fallen humanity to victory again.

Life in a Fallen World: The Hope of Victory

This passage teaches us several important truths that we must understand to combat the devil. First, Satan "wears" camouflage and does not reveal his true identity. Satan is as cunning as a snake who sometimes comes as an "angel of light" or a wolf in sheep's clothing (2 Cor 11:4; Matt 7:15). Second, while the outcome of the war sometimes seems to be in doubt, the certainty of God's victory is foretold at the very beginning (Gen 3:15). One from the seed of the woman would crush the head of the serpent. When you feel overcome with hopelessness, remember God through Christ has won the victory. Praise him for what he has accomplished on your behalf. Thank him that truth is not determined by how you feel, but by what God's Word says. His Word is always true.

Third, the serpent's challenge and distortion of God's Word remain two of Satan's chief strategies. While false teaching is a constant danger to God's people, God has given us his Word in written form. God's Word—read, studied, memorized, meditated on, and applied—is an effective weapon against the schemes of the enemy (Matt 4:1–11; Eph 6:11).

Fourth, the world and the flesh and the devil will continually seek to get Christians to believe that God does not have their best interest at heart. The enemy wants Christians to believe that God is withholding "the good life" from them. Yet the truth is that the devil comes only to steal, kill, and destroy. By contrast, Jesus came that we may experience abundant life (John 10:10).

Finally, we must consider the fact that Jesus is the greater and second Adam. Jesus undid what Adam did when Adam sinned against God. The contrast between the first and second Adam is striking. While the first Adam ate from a forbidden tree, Jesus (the second Adam) died on a forsaken tree (Deut 21:23). While Adam and Eve were punished for their sin against God, Jesus (the second Adam) bore the punishment of God's wrath on the cross for the sins of others. After the first Adam died, his body decomposed in a tomb, but after Jesus (the second Adam) died, his body was raised from the dead!

Life in a Fallen World: A Theology of Thorns

Despite Satan's various attempts to undermine God's work, Satan never defeats God. One example of victory despite Satan's work is found in 1 Thess 2:17–18. Paul wrote, "But as for us, brothers and sisters, after we were forced to leave you for a short time (in person, not in heart), we greatly desired and made every effort to return and see you face to face. So we wanted to come to you—even I, Paul, time and again—but Satan hindered us."

We do not know how Satan hindered Paul's return to Thessalonica, but Paul clearly attributes the roadblock to Satan.[12] One might understand Paul's words to describe an instance where Satan outmaneuvered God, but that would fail to see the bigger picture. For example, Paul's inability to return to Thessalonica resulted in his writing two letters to the Thessalonian believers which became a part of the New Testament. If Paul had returned to Thessalonica, it is not likely he would have needed to write these two letters.

Second, Paul's inability to return to Thessalonica resulted in his eighteen months' stay in Corinth (Acts 18:1–18). While Corinth was hardly a perfect church, Paul left behind a solid

---

[12] This discussion is based on my work in Cook and Lawless, *Spiritual Warfare in the Storyline of Scripture*, 100–101.

work—due in part to his lengthy stay—when he departed
the church at the conclusion of his second missionary journey. Consequently, when you feel like life has hemmed you in
or Satan has kept you from experiencing God's best for you,
remember God is never outwitted by Satan. Trust God has you
where he wants you to be. Ask yourself, "How can I live for God
and glorify him right now?" God wants to use you "in Corinth"
even though you'd like to be "in Thessalonica."

Another example of God sovereignly using Satan to accomplish his purposes is Paul's "thorn in the flesh" (2 Cor 12:7–10).[13]
In the passage, Paul described his thorn in the flesh as simultane-
ously a "messenger of Satan" and something God gave him. The
words "was given" should be interpreted as a divine passive and
understood as coming from God (v. 7). What Satan meant for
evil, God meant for good (cf. Gen 50:20).[14]

In the passage, the apostle draws a contrast between his heavenly visions (vv. 1–6) and his thorn in the flesh (v. 7). Paul asked
God on three occasions to remove the thorn from him. While
God did not elect to remove the thorn, God did use it in Paul's
life to keep him humble and dependent on Christ. Paul could
have easily become proud because of his visions and revelations,

---

[13] For a more complete discussion on Paul's thorn in the flesh, see
Cook and Lawless, *Spiritual Warfare in the Storyline of Scripture*, 131;
George H. Guthrie, *2 Corinthians*, Baker Exegetical Commentary on the
New Testament (Grand Rapids: Baker, 2015), 589.

[14] For a thoroughgoing discussion of God's purposeful sovereignty over
Satan and demons, see John Piper, *Providence* (Wheaton, IL: Crossway,
2020), 255–84. For a similarly extensive treatment of the problem of evil,
see Scott Christensen, *What about Evil? A Defense of God's Sovereign Glory*
(Phillipsburg, NJ: P&R, 2020).

but his thorn kept him humble. Thus, God used Satan to accomplish his purpose in Paul's life.

Here a word of caution is in order for all church leaders: when God uses people, it is easy for them to begin to make their ministry more about themselves than about God. One way you can see pride taking hold in leaders' ministerial lives is by the way they treat others. If they speak to others in ways they would never allow others to speak to them, then pride may very well have taken root in their hearts.

Pride can also be seen when one takes great offense for not being credited for what God does through them. Therefore, do not begrudge God for appointing a thorn in your life to keep you humble because "'God opposes the proud but gives grace to the humble'" (Jas 4:6 ESV, citing Prov 3:34). God appoints the humbling thorns in our lives as means of his all-sufficient grace.

Redemption: Crushing the Serpent at the Cross

While the biblical teaching concerning Christ's death focuses primarily on his accomplishment of salvation from God's wrath against sin, the cross also dealt the devil a fatal blow.[15] Jesus Christ decisively crushed the serpent's head *at the cross*. At times

---

[15] Stott discusses this "conquest of evil" as an additional achievement of the cross. John R. W. Stott, *The Cross of Christ* (Downers Grove, IL: InterVarsity, 2006), 223–46; Treat argues that, according to Scripture, Jesus's victory over Satan is accomplished through Jesus's penal substitutionary death. Thus, the latter is the necessary and sufficient means by which the former is accomplished. Jeremy R. Treat, *The Crucified King: Atonement and Kingdom in Biblical and Systematic Theology* (Grand Rapids: Zondervan, 2014).

the outcome of the war between God and the devil seems to be in doubt from a human perspective, but from a divine vantage point, God's victory is certain (Gen 3:15). In addition, Christ's death on the cross also humiliated God's supernatural enemies— Satan and his demons.

According to Paul

An important passage highlighting God's victory and humiliation of the forces of darkness is Col 2:14–15 (cf. Col 1:12–14). The verses read, "He erased the certificate of debt, with its obligations, that was against us and opposed to us, and has taken it away by nailing it to the cross. He disarmed the rulers and authorities and disgraced them publicly; he triumphed over them in him."

While v. 14 teaches the believers' forgiveness of sin was accomplished at the cross, v. 15 expands on the defeat and humiliation of the "rulers and authorities." These "rulers and authorities" refer to demonic spirits at work in the world (cf. 1:13–16; Eph 2:2; 3:10; 6:12).[16] These fallen spirits have been rendered ineffective in their war against Christ and his people.

The Greek word translated "disarmed" is used in Col 3:9 in the sense of "strip off," as one casts aside a dirty piece of clothing. While the devil and his demonic minions are not totally divested of their power in this age, they no longer have the influence and

---

[16] The reference is likely inclusive of both. For this reading in Colossians, see, e.g., G. K. Beale, *Colossians and Philemon*, Baker Exegetical Commentary on the New Testament (Grand Rapids: Baker, 2019), 181–82, 198–204.

authority over Christians they had before their conversion. Why? Because, when believers are forgiven (that is, their debt has been paid by Christ), Satan's grounds for accusation and degradation are removed.

Furthermore, Christ humiliated his enemies by making a "a public spectacle of them." Ironically, at the precise moment the world and the forces of evil were shaming and humiliating Christ according to their own standards, according to Paul just the opposite was true according to God's standards—in his death, Christ put them to public shame.[17] Paul's words remind believers they have nothing to fear. Jesus has conquered the forces of hell, and we share in his victory over them.

According to John

A more dramatic presentation of Christ's victory over Satan at the cross is found in Revelation 12. This apocalyptic passage takes readers behind the scenes of human history and allows them to peek into the spiritual realm. The passage depicts Satan's defeat at the cross and his hatred for the church. The heart of the passage for our consideration is vv. 7–12:

> Then war broke out in heaven: Michael and his angels fought against the dragon. The dragon and his angels also fought, but he could not prevail, and there was no place for them in heaven any longer. So the great dragon

---

[17] See Beale, *Colossians and Philemon*, 202–4. On this inversion of the honor/shame paradigm, see David A. deSilva, *Honor, Patronage, Kinship & Purity: Unlocking New Testament Culture* (Downers Grove, IL: InterVarsity, 2000), 51–61.

was thrown out—the ancient serpent, who is called the devil and Satan, the one who deceives the whole world. He was thrown to earth, and his angels with him. Then I heard a loud voice in heaven say,

The salvation and the power
and the kingdom of our God
and the authority of his Christ
have now come,
because the accuser of our brothers and sisters,
who accuses them
before our God day and night,
has been thrown down.
They conquered him
by the blood of the Lamb
and by the word of their testimony;
for they did not love their lives
to the point of death.
Therefore rejoice, you heavens,
and you who dwell in them!
Woe to the earth and the sea,
because the devil has come down to you
with great fury,
because he knows his time is short.

John makes it perfectly clear that the great red dragon and the serpent in the garden are none other than the devil himself (v. 9). The apocalyptic war fought in heaven is interpreted by "a loud voice in heaven" (v. 10). Satan, the accuser of the people of God, is cast out of heaven because of the shed blood of the Lamb (vv. 10–11). New Testament scholar Tom Schreiner astutely observes:

Believers *conquer* because "the Lion from the tribe of Judah . . . has *conquered*" ([Rev] 5:5). Our victory is rooted in his victory; Christ's death on the cross is the basis for the triumph of the saints. We have an apocalyptic version here [in Rev 12:7–12] of what we read in John 12:31, where Jesus anticipates that at his death, "the ruler of this world"—Satan—"[will] be cast out" (Gk. *ekblēthēsetai*). In Revelation 12, the verb is "throw out" (Gk. *ballō*), but the concept is the same. The serpent, the devil, Satan, the mighty dragon has been ejected from heaven, but his defeat comes not through overwhelming force, nor even by the strength of Michael, but through the suffering and death of the Son of God.[18]

Just as we saw in Colossians, because Christ's death paid the penalty for believers' sins, Satan can no longer bring accusations against them. Previously, Satan was permitted into God's presence, where he would accuse God's people day and night (Job 1:6–9; 2:1–6; Zech 3:1–2). Revelation 12 concludes with a depiction of Satan's current work. Satan (the dragon) is warring against God's people: "So the dragon was furious with the woman [the church] and went off to wage war against the rest of her offspring—those who keep the commands of God and hold firmly to the testimony about Jesus" (12:17). But, as we saw above, Satan's evil intentions are governed and made to serve our good by our Creator and Redeemer.

---

[18] Thomas R. Schreiner, *The Joy of Hearing: A Theology of the Book of Revelation*, New Testament Theology (Wheaton, IL: Crossway, 2021), 132.

Sharing in Victory

Christ's supernatural enemies are powerless against him. Believers share in Christ's victory because of their union with Christ.[19] The following verses confirm the thought of a believer's participation in Christ's victory over the enemy:

- Romans 8:37–39: "No, in all these things we are more than conquerors through him who loved us. For I am persuaded that neither death nor life, nor angels nor rulers, nor things present nor things to come, nor powers, nor height nor depth, nor any other created thing will be able to separate us from the love of God that is in Christ Jesus our Lord."
- Romans 16:20: "The God of peace will soon crush Satan under your feet. The grace of our Lord Jesus be with you."
- 1 Corinthians 15:24–25: "Then comes the end, when he hands over the kingdom to God the Father, when he abolishes all rule and all authority and power. For he must reign until he puts all his enemies under his feet."
- 1 Corinthians 15:57: "But thanks be to God, who gives us the victory though our Lord Jesus Christ!"
- Galatians 1:4: ". . . who gave himself for our sins to rescue us from this present evil age, according to the will of our God and Father."
- Colossians 1:12–14: ". . . giving thanks to the Father, who has enabled you to share in the saints' inheritance in

---

[19] For an accessible yet thorough discussion of union with Christ, see Robert Letham, *Union with Christ: In Scripture, History, and Theology* (Phillipsburg, NJ: P&R, 2011).

the light. He has rescued us from the domain of darkness and transferred us into the kingdom of the Son he loves. In him we have redemption, the forgiveness of sins."

- 1 John 3:8: "The Son of God was revealed for this purpose: to destroy the devil's works."
- 1 John 4:4: "You are from God, little children, and you have conquered them, because the one who is in you is greater than the one who is in the world."

Read these verses aloud, study them in their context, and meditate on their meaning and significance because the Holy Spirit uses the Word of God to strengthen believers' faith. That Word declares the truth which forms our belt (Eph 6:14a), displays the righteousness which is our breastplate (6:14b), presents the gospel which shods our feet (6:15), bolsters the faith which forms our shield (6:16), offers the salvation which safeguards our souls (6:17), and furnishes us as the most formidable spiritual weapon (6:17). This Word prayerfully employed enables the Christian to stand firm against the schemes of the devil (6:18, 11).

Consummation: At the End of All Things

Briefly, we turn our attention to the devil's final judgment in the lake of fire (Rev 20:10). The passage reads, "The devil who deceived them was thrown into the lake of fire and sulfur where the beast and the false prophet are, and they will be tormented day and night forever and ever."

This verse paints a brief but dramatic picture of the destiny of God's archenemy, the devil. In graphic imagery, Satan is thrown into the lake of fire *forever*. Never again will Satan deceive the nations. Never again will Satan and his demons tempt the people of God. Never again will Satan instigate persecution against the church. Never again will the devil use heartache and suffering against God's people. Although the nations rage and peoples plot in vain (Ps 2:1; Acts 4:25), Revelation provides a window into the spiritual dynamics at play and assures us that those who listen to and heed God's Word will conquer because the Lamb has conquered.[20]

What Satan Doesn't Want You to Know

Believers must never forget that Jesus Christ defeated the devil and his demons at the cross. As a result of Christ's victory over Satan, believers share in that victory because of their union with Christ. Christians have absolutely no reason to fear Satan and his demons. Greater is the Holy Spirit in the lives of believers than the one (Satan) who is in the world (1 John 4:4). Yet we must remain vigilant against the attacks of the enemy, not underestimating a wicked foe who has nothing to lose. Christians must be alert to Satan's schemes and subtle attacks.

---

[20] We recommend Schreiner's overview of the forces of evil in Revelation (*The Joy of Hearing*, 31–45). He concludes, "Government may gobble up human rights in the name of justice, and Christians may find themselves in the situation described by John, in which they face discrimination in employment, are persecuted, or are even put to death. Such economic and political discrimination opens up the temptation to compromise with the world, and John warns believers about this mortal danger. . . . We must not shut our eyes to the true nature of the battle being waged, nor should we be deceived, as if any political program will instantiate the kingdom of God" (45).

Your Identity

Consider who God says you are because of your union with Christ. Paul states in Col 2:9–10, "For the entire fullness of God's nature dwells bodily in Christ, and you have been filled by him, who is the head over every ruler and authority." Arnold explains the thought of the passage this way, "Paul connected the Colossians' possession of 'divine fullness' with Christ's supremacy to the demonic powers."[21] Believers are filled with the fullness of Christ and, thereby, have the power and authority to defeat Satan and his demons in spiritual warfare. Many believers do not understand who they are in Christ and, consequently, struggle against the powers of this dark age.

Satan does not want Christians to understand their new identity *in Christ*. He is delighted when they, like the world, find their identity elsewhere—whether in their sexuality, skin color, career, family, sports team, favorite video game, academic guild, social club, or otherwise. Whatever you fancy, so long as it is unhinged from Christ, Satan will work with that. Therefore, you should read and pray over the verses listed below to allow the Holy Spirit to solidify in your heart the truth about your identity in Christ.

We have stated the verses in a form as if spoken directly to you. The following is just a sample list of who you are in Christ and the blessings that are yours because of your union with Christ. You might even use each statement to confess with gratitude who you are in Christ:[22]

---

[21] Clinton E. Arnold, *Powers of Darkness: Principalities & Powers in Paul's Letters* (Downers Grove, IL: InterVarsity, 1992), 116.

[22] We are indebted to Neil Anderson for this idea. Neil T. Anderson, *The Bondage Breaker* (Eugene, OR: Harvest House, 1990).

- You have been born again to a living hope (1 Pet 1:3).
- You are a child of God (John 1:12; 1 John 3:1).
- You are a saint (Phil 1:1).
- You have a protected salvation (1 Pet 1:4–5).
- You are a new creation (2 Cor 5:17).
- You have been bought with a price (2 Cor 6:10).
- You are washed, sanctified, and justified by the blood of Jesus (1 Cor 6:11).
- You are God's temple (1 Cor 3:16).
- You are more than a conqueror through Christ (Rom 8:37).
- Nothing can separate you from the love of God (Rom 8:39).
- The Holy Spirit intercedes for you (Rom 8:27).
- You are being conformed into the image of Christ (Rom 8:29).
- God causes all things to work together for your good (Rom 8:28).
- You are indwelt by the Holy Spirit (Rom 8:9).
- You are no longer a slave to sin (Rom 6:17).
- You are free from condemnation (Rom 8:1).
- You have eternal life in Christ Jesus (Rom 6:23).
- You're alive to God and dead to sin (Rom 6:11).
- Your old self was crucified with Christ (Rom 6:6).
- You have been baptized into Christ's death and raised to walk in newness of life (Rom 6:3–4).
- Your citizenship is in heaven (Phil 3:20).
- God has begun a good work in you, and he will complete it (Phil 1:6).
- You are a child of light (Eph 5:8).

- You are the salt of the earth (Matt 5:13).
- You are the light of the world (Matt 5:14).
- You are blessed with every spiritual blessing in Christ (Eph 1:3).
- You were chosen by God before the creation of the world (Eph 1:4).
- If you ask for anything in Jesus's name, he will do it (John 14:16).
- You have been raised with Christ and are seated with him in the heavenlies (Eph 2:6).
- You have been saved by grace through faith (Eph 2:8).
- God loves you, just as he loves Jesus (John 17:23).
- You are redeemed from the curse of the law (Gal 5:13).
- You have been crucified with Christ, and Christ now lives his life through you (Gal 2:20).
- You are an ambassador for Christ (2 Cor 5:20).
- You are kept from the evil one (John 17:15).
- You are part of God's gracious gift to Jesus (John 17:6).
- You have peace with God (Rom 5:1).
- You have been justified by faith (Rom 5:1).
- You have been transferred out of Satan's kingdom and into Christ's kingdom (Col 1:13).
- You are forgiven of all your transgressions (Eph 1:7).

So many more verses could be added, but the point is that Christians are not who the devil wants them to think they are.[23] These truths give believers a better understanding of their

---

[23] For a superb resource to regularly remind ourselves who we are in Christ, we highly recommend acquiring Milton Vincent, *A Gospel Primer: For Christians* (Bemidji, MN: Focus, 2008).

identity in Christ. Satan wants us to define ourselves apart from our relationship to God.

The Daily Battle and the Eternal Victory

Remember, James offers a magnificent promise: if believers resist the devil, he will flee. The context of the command is crucial for understanding how one is to resist the devil, so it bears citing again: "Therefore, submit to God. Resist the devil, and he will flee from you. Draw near to God, and he will draw near to you" (Jas 4:7–8).

Obedience to Christ is not always easy; that is why temptation is considered spiritual warfare. Resistance begins by submitting to God's revealed will in Scripture, including taking God's perspective on our identity. Resistance says no to temptations by drawing near to God—turning one's attention to God through praying, worshiping, donning the armor of God, and recalling the truths of Scripture. This does not mean that the resistance will not be prolonged and intense—indeed, unless Christ returns, you must resist your entire momentary life (2 Cor 4:16–17; Jas 1:11; 4:14).

While the devil wants you to think you can have "your best life now" perspective, God's Word provides an eternal perspective. You are a child of God, indwelt by God's Spirit, clothed in Christ's righteousness, and have open access to God's presence. If that's the case, what more do we need? An eternity without any spiritual battles to fight is waiting for God's people to enjoy. Armed with a biblical perspective on your identity and eternity, you stand better equipped to resist the devil.

Conclusion

We have started this book with this look at our enemy, the devil. But we will continue to remind you the Bible is not a book about the devil. The Bible does not answer every question we might have about Satan and his forces. Novelists have offered their own descriptions, and theologians have at times proposed ideas. The Bible, though, tells us what we need to know: the devil is real, but he is a defeated foe. With that truth in mind, we proceed in the next chapter to "the world," the second enemy we face.

CHAPTER 2

Do Not Love the World

John Bunyan's famous allegory, *Pilgrim's Progress*, depicts the journey of the main character, Christian, on his way to the Celestial City.[1] Although the story was written in the seventeenth century, the book remains a powerful depiction of the alluring nature of worldliness. For example, Christian must pass through a place called "Vanity," which holds a fair called "Vanity Fair." This fair was created by the devil and his servants because the way to the Celestial City passed through the center of Vanity in such a way that all pilgrims would have to travel through it.

In Bunyan's allegory, Vanity Fair symbolizes the captivating nature of the world and its opposition to those headed to heaven. The fair is something akin to an ancient flea market, presenting

---

[1] *The Pilgrim's Progress* was first published in 1678 and 1684. For a more current version, see John Bunyan, *The Pilgrim's Progress* (Wheaton, IL: Crossway, 2019).

anything and everything the world has to offer. This place and its inhabitants whisper into people's ears, suggesting fleshly pleasures are more satisfying than God himself. People passing through Vanity Fair are encouraged to seize the day (*carpe diem*), enjoy themselves, and consider God tomorrow; however, for most, tomorrow is always one more day away. Vanity Fair, therefore, is Bunyan's attempt to warn his audience about the dangers of the worldliness of the world.

The World Revealed

In the Bible, the classic text on not loving the world is 1 John 2:15–17. The passage reads, "Do not love the world or the things in the world. If anyone loves the world, the love of the Father is not in him. For everything in the world—the lust of the flesh, the lust of the eyes, and the pride in one's possessions—is not from the Father, but is from the world. And the world with its lust is passing away, but the one who does the will of God remains forever."

What did John mean by "Do not love the world"? This phrase is a divinely inspired imperative that we must obey, so the question is important—especially since John also wrote in what may be the most famous verse in the Bible (John 3:16) that God *loves the world.* Either "loving the world" is something only God can do, or John used the term "world" in different senses.

Obviously, the term "world" has various nuances, from the created universe to the world of people, or as the term is used in 1 John 2:15–16, humanity in rebellion against God and under the dominion of Satan.[2] But the world is more than just humanity

---

[2] Hendriksen provides a helpful taxonomy of John's use of *kosmos* (world) in his Gospel. He identifies six uses: "(1) the (orderly) universe,

under Satan's dominion. Clinton Arnold makes this clear: "*The world* is the unhealthy social environment in which we live. This includes the ungodly aspects of culture, peer pressure, values, traditions, 'what is in,' 'what is uncool,' customs, philosophies, and attitudes. The world represents the prevailing worldview assumptions of the day that stand contrary to the biblical understanding of reality and biblical values."[3]

Later in 1 John, the apostle writes that "the whole world is under the sway of the evil one" (5:19). Several times in the Fourth Gospel, John refers to Satan as the "ruler of this world" (12:31; 14:30; 16:11). The world is Satan's realm of influence and dominance. Christians are those who are in the world but not of the world (John 17:11).

Paul made a similar point when he told the Galatians they had been rescued "from this present evil age" (Gal 1:4). The thought of rescue suggests that one is helpless and can do nothing to rescue oneself. Before one is rescued by Christ, he or she is in bondage

---

[John] 17:5; perhaps, the earth, 21:25. (2) by metonymy, the human inhabitants of the earth; hence, mankind, realm of mankind, human race, theatre of human history, framework of human society. 16:21. (3) the general public, 7:4; perhaps also 14:22. (4) ethical sense: mankind alienated from the life of God, sin-laden, exposed to the judgment, in the need of salvation, 3:19. (5) the same as (4) with the additional idea that no distinction is made with respect to race or nationality; hence, men from every tribe and nation; not only Jews but also Gentiles, 4:42 and probably also 1:29; 3:16, 17; 6:33, 51; 8:12; 9:5; 12:46; 1 John 2:2; 4:14, 15. Such passages should be read in the light of 4:42; 11:52; and 12:32. . . . (6) the realm of evil. This is really the same as (4) but with the additional idea of open hostility to God, his Christ, and his people 7:7; 8:23; 12:31; 14:30; 15:18; 17:9, 14." William W. Hendriksen, *Exposition of the Gospel according to John*, 2 vols., *New Testament Commentary* (Grand Rapids: Baker, 1953), 1:79n26.

[3] Arnold, *3 Crucial Questions about Spiritual Warfare*, 34, italics in original (see chap. 1, n. 2).

to the prince of this world. One is held captive in the "present evil age." Thus, the "world" in 1 John 2:15–17 can refer to both people under Satan's dominion and the system of evil that holds them captive. David Wells describes the world's sway over fallen humanity:

> It is one of the defining marks of Our Time that God is now weightless. I do not mean by this that he is ethereal but rather that he has become unimportant. He rests upon the world as inconsequentially as not to be noticeable. He has lost his saliency for human life. Those who assure the pollsters of their belief in God's existence may nonetheless consider him less interesting than television, his commands less authoritative than their appetites for affluence and influence, his judgments no more awe-inspiring than the evening news, and his truth less compelling than the advertisers' sweet fog of flattery and lies.[4]

The world under Satan's dominance manifests itself in the promotion of godless cultures and worldviews. The prince of this world uses the enticement of the world to seduce people further and further away from God. In fact, John pulls back the curtain on the world and exposes Satan's dominion for what it truly is—a prostitute riding on the back of a beast (Rev 17–18). As Ray Ortlund writes, "The 'great harlot' [is] the embodiment of human society fully given over to the lust of the flesh and the lust of the eyes and the pride of life."[5] While Revelation 17 and

---

[4] David F. Wells, *God in the Wasteland: The Reality of Truth in a World of Fading Dreams* (Grand Rapids: Eerdmans, 1994), 88.

[5] Raymond C. Ortlund, *God's Unfaithful Wife: A Biblical Theology of Spiritual Adultery*, New Studies in Biblical Theology 2 (Downers Grove, IL: InterVarsity, 2002), 161.

18 are apocalyptic pictures of Satan's end-time kingdom, what is true at the end of human history is equally true at the present time. Although the imagery is clearly apocalyptic, its meaning is relatively clear: herein, the world is revealed.

As a Prostitute

The image of a prostitute is shocking and grotesque. The prostitute stands in sharp contrast to the bride of the Lamb described in Revelation 21.[6] The bride is presented in all her purity and represents the church of Jesus Christ. The prostitute, however, is clothed in a manner intended to entice the unsuspecting. The passage reads:

> Then one of the seven angels who had the seven bowls came and spoke with me: "Come, I will show you the judgment of the notorious prostitute who is seated on many waters. The kings of the earth committed sexual immorality with her, and those who live on the earth became drunk on the wine of her sexual immorality." Then he carried me away in the Spirit to a wilderness. I saw a woman sitting on a scarlet beast that was covered with blasphemous names and had seven heads and ten horns. The woman was dressed in purple and scarlet, adorned with gold, jewels, and pearls. She had a golden cup in her hand filled with everything detestable and with the impurities of her prostitution. On her forehead was written a name, a mystery: Babylon the Great, the

---

[6] On this comparison, see Brian J. Tabb, *All Things New: Revelation as Canonical Capstone*, New Studies in Biblical Theology 48 (Downers Grove, IL: InterVarsity, 2019), 163–86.

Mother of Prostitutes and of the Detestable Things of the Earth. Then I saw that the woman was drunk with the blood of the saints and with the blood of the witnesses to Jesus. (Rev 17:1–6)

The prostitute is described as having significant economic influence over the world ("who is seated on many waters," v. 1). She uses her power to promote idolatry (the worship of anything or anyone other than God), though no doubt sexual promiscuity would not be discouraged. The Old Testament is replete with descriptions of Israel's infidelity to the Lord as spiritual harlotry (Jer 3:1–3; Ezek 16; 23; Hos 2:5; 4:10–12, 18; 5:3–4; 6:10; 9:1).[7] Money, sex, and power are three of Satan's most powerful temptations to keep people from turning to Christ.

Furthermore, the prostitute is responsible for the persecution of God's people, as she is drunk on the blood of the saints. To grasp this horrific imagery, we must remember that blood is the seat of life (Lev 17:11–14), and to take blood is to take away life.[8] The image of the harlot drinking blood, therefore, reveals that the world—though it offers all who will listen their "best life now," like Vanity Fair—promotes not virtuous life but a culture of death. The dominion of darkness (the world) appears innocuous, but the world is in fact nothing less than a deceptive prostitute seducing people into everlasting judgment.

---

[7] The Old Testament references are from Schreiner, whose succinct discussion of the harlot is quite helpful. Schreiner, *The Joy of Hearing*, 40–41 (see chap. 1, n. 18). The theme of spiritual adultery is given full treatment in Ortlund, *God's Unfaithful Wife*.

[8] See the thorough discussion in Leon Morris, *The Apostolic Preaching of the Cross*, 3rd ed. (Grand Rapids: Eerdmans, 1965), 112–28. Morris aptly wrote that the term *blood* is used not typically to speak of *life being available* in some mystic sense but of "life *violently taken*" (121, emphasis added).

John's description of the world explains why James equates friendship with the world to being an enemy of God (Jas 4:4). Those who love the world are committing adultery against God. Adultery is the ultimate betrayal in a marriage relationship. The use of the term reveals how terrible worldliness in a person's life is.

Each individual must decide whether he or she will love the harlot of Revelation 17 or the bride in Revelation 21. The person following the path of least resistance—the broad way of destruction—walks like an ox to the slaughter to the prostitute (Prov 7:22), but whoever listens to God's Word (9:4–6; Isa 55:1–3; John 6:27; Rev 22:17), following the difficult road—the narrow way that leads to life—will face resistance from the world, the flesh, and the devil (1 Pet 4:1–6). While the right decision seems obvious, the allurement of the world seduces the unsuspecting.

As an Empire

Revelation 18 paints a similar portrait of the world by using the image of an impregnable city rather than a prostitute. Revelation 18:1–3 depicts this city:

> After this I saw another angel with great authority coming down from heaven, and the earth was illuminated by his splendor. He called out in a mighty voice:
>
> It has fallen,
> Babylon the Great has fallen!
> She has become a home for demons,
> a haunt for every unclean spirit,
> a haunt for every unclean bird,

and a haunt for every unclean and despicable beast.
For all the nations have drunk
the wine of her sexual immorality,
which brings wrath.
The kings of the earth
have committed sexual immorality with her,
and the merchants of the earth
have grown wealthy from her sensuality and excess.

The very things the unredeemed heart longs for this city offers. The city is ancient Babylon, the great enemy of God's people. In John's day, the city represented Rome. Yet more than just a city is depicted here. An apocalyptic picture of the dominion of Satan is portrayed. The city is characterized by political power, extraordinary artistry, and unfathomable wealth. From a human perspective, the city seems invincible and its alluring façade irresistible. One could easily become intoxicated by the might and splendor of such a godless city, after all, by her "merchants . . . have grown wealthy" (v. 3). There is much to gain financially in this life from loving the world and everything to lose in the next (Mark 8:36). The truth, however, is that the world is nothing more than a prostitute dressed in fanciful garb. The world is little more than a city offering any and every pleasure a person desires.

Do Not Love the World

We have taken this detour from 1 John 2:15–17, mentioned at the outset of this chapter, so that we could see how truly dangerous and horrible it is "to love the world." When John tells his readers, "Do not love the world," he does *not* mean they are to love neither people nor creation. We should then ask what John does intend his readers to understand by these three phrases. John is specific in what he means by the world: "all that is in the world, the lust of the flesh, the lust of the eyes, and the boastful pride of life" (NASB). The word translated "lust" may also be translated "desire" (ESV) or "coveting" (as in Rom 7:7–8; cf. Exod 20:17 in the Greek Old Testament, "You shall not covet your neighbor's wife"). While the term "lust" does not always have a negative connotation, it clearly does in this context.

Lust of the Flesh

The "lust of the flesh" describes the longings that arise by virtue of being fallen in Adam.[9] While John does not predominantly use the term "flesh" in precisely the same way Paul commonly uses the term, in this instance there is likely much overlap (e.g., Paul's "works of the flesh" [Gal 5:19–21] or "liv[ing] according to the flesh" [Rom 8:13]).[10] John's phrase seems identical to what Paul means by the "deceitful desires" of our "old self" in Ephesians 4:22 (see also Col 3:9; Rom 6:6; Gal 5:24). The mindset that characterizes the old self, Paul says in Rom 8:6–7, "is death . . . is hostile to God because it does not submit to God's

---

[9] On the fall and sin in the biblical storyline, see Christopher W. Morgan, "Sin in the Biblical Story," in *Fallen: A Theology of Sin*, ed. Christopher W. Morgan, Theology in Community (Wheaton, IL: Crossway, 2013), 131–62.

[10] For overviews of flesh in Paul, see Thomas R. Schreiner, *Paul, Apostle of God's Glory in Christ: A Pauline Theology*, 1st ed. (Downers Grove, IL: InterVarsity, 2001), 141–46; Douglas J. Moo, *A Theology of Paul and His Letters: The Gift of the New Realm in Christ*, Biblical Theology of the New Testament (Grand Rapids: Zondervan, 2021), 452–54.

law." Someone in the grip of the "lust of the flesh" is hostile to God, refusing to submit to his authority in certain areas of life.

That John has something similar in mind is embedded in 1 John 2:15, "If anyone loves the world, the love of the Father is not in him." When he speaks of the "love of the Father," we must ask whether the genitive, "of the Father," is objective (i.e., believer's love for the Father) or subjective (i.e., the Father's love for a believer). New Testament scholar Bob Yarbrough convincingly argues for the former:

> The person who sets affection on the world cannot exercise true love for the Father. There are two reasons for this. First, authentic love for the Father requires reception of God's love as revealed in his Son through the cross: "This is love: not that we loved God, but that he loved us and sent his Son as an atoning sacrifice for our sins" (1 John 4:10 NIV). The love for the Father that John is thinking of is not a natural affection innate to all people, but a gracious enablement brought about by the gospel. For there to be "love for the Father" (objective genitive), there must be a prior "love by the Father" (subjective genitive) received by a sinner. . . . Second, authentic love for God exists only when it has no essential rivals. . . . To attempt to love God in multitasking fashion, dedicating a portion of one's love worldward and then the remaining amount godward, is fruitless because it fails to acknowledge God as he truly is: sole, unique, sovereign, alone deserving one's core allegiance.[11]

---

[11] Robert W. Yarbrough, *1–3 John*, Baker Exegetical Commentary on the New Testament (Grand Rapids: Baker, 2008), 130.

Therefore, the person loving the "lust of the flesh" stands in hostility to God and does not submit to him because love for the Father is lacking.

Lust of the Eyes

An organic connection exists between the lust of the flesh and that of the eyes. The lust of the eyes is a way of describing sinful desires initiated or inflamed by what one sees and results in feelings of envy and coveting.

We see examples of the "lust of the eyes" in the sin of Eve in the garden: "The woman *saw* that the tree was good for food and delightful to look at, and that it was desirable for obtaining wisdom" (Gen 3:6, italics added). The same was true for Achan after the invasion of the Promised Land: "Achan replied to Joshua, 'It is true. I have sinned against the LORD, the God of Israel. This is what I did: When I *saw* among the spoils a beautiful cloak from Babylon, five pounds of silver, and a bar of gold weighing a pound and a quarter, I *coveted* them and took them'" (Josh 7:20–21, italics added).

A third tragic example is David's sin against God in his adultery with Bathsheba. David's move toward adultery began when he remained at home instead of accompanying his troops into battle. On a sleepless night, David ventured onto his balcony and saw Bathsheba bathing. Instead, immediately returning indoors, he stood and fixed his gaze upon her. The sad episode reads, "While he was on the roof, he *saw* a woman bathing. She was very beautiful. So David sent his servants to find out who she was. A servant answered, 'That woman is Bathsheba daughter of Eliam. She is the wife of Uriah the

Hittite.' So David sent messengers to bring Bathsheba to him. When she came to him, he had sexual relations with her" (2 Sam 11:2–4 NCV, italics added).

Paul may have had this episode in mind when he told the Corinthians, "Flee sexual immorality!" (1 Cor 6:18). Jesus addressed the same issue: "You have heard that it was said, 'Do not commit adultery.' But I tell you, everyone who looks at a woman lustfully has already committed adultery with her in his heart. If your right eye causes you to sin, gouge it out and throw it away. For it is better that you lose one of the parts of your body than for your whole body to be thrown into hell" (Matt 5:27–29). Jesus's use of hyperbole ("If your right eye is causing you to sin, gouge it out") reveals how dangerous sexual lust can be to a person. Adultery normally begins with the lust of the eyes. The same is true, in fact, of almost all sexual sin.

Jesus's point is that believers must deal decisively and seriously with temptation. To gouge out the eye may mean, if you struggle with internet pornography, you get rid of your computer, or at the very least, install a program on it that will allow somebody else to see every website you search. To gouge out your eye may mean that you cannot keep your television channels, streaming services, or other entertainment platforms if you are tempted either to view ungodly content or to "binge watch" something to the neglect of your family, work, schoolwork, or otherwise. Again, Jesus's point is not to offer a list of legalistic rules and regulations, but to admonish his followers to deal ruthlessly with the source of temptation. You do not weed your garden by trimming the leaves of the parasitic plant to make it prettier—you pull them out by the roots!

Pride of One's Possessions

Finally, John refers to the "boastful pride of life" (1 John 2:16 NASB). The term translated "pride" normally refers to one who is arrogant and conceited (cf. ASV: "vainglory"). The term translated "life" (*bios*) is not John's usual term for life (*zōē*, as in 1:2), and it is used later in 1 John with reference to material possessions (3:17). Therefore, John is speaking about one's arrogance and sense of self-importance tied to their possessions and status.

Jesus dealt with such a person when he encountered the rich young ruler (Luke 18:18–22). The young man chose his wealth over following Jesus. In the ensuing discussion, Jesus said, "How hard it is for those who have wealth to enter the kingdom of God! For it is easier for a camel to go through the eye of a needle than for a rich person to enter the kingdom of God" (Luke 18:24–25). The disciples were stunned by Jesus's comment and wondered who could be saved (Luke 18:26). Paul made a similar comment to the Corinthians:

> Brothers and sisters, consider your calling: Not many were wise from a human perspective, not many powerful, not many of noble birth. Instead, God has chosen what is foolish in the world to shame the wise, and God has chosen what is weak in the world to shame the strong. God has chosen what is insignificant and despised in the world—what is viewed as nothing—to bring to nothing what is viewed as something, so that no one may boast in his presence. (1 Cor 1:26–29)

Wealth and influence can blind a person to the need for Christ. We need to hear Paul's rebuking question, "What do you have that you didn't receive? If, in fact, you did receive it, why do you boast as if you hadn't received it?" (1 Cor 4:7). Boasting about skill or possessions is rooted in the neglect of our Creator as the all-sufficient Giver, and—audaciously—it seeks to receive the glory due to God. Yet, in spite of this, as Jesus went on to say, "What is impossible with man is possible with God" (Luke 18:27). Jesus can thread the camel through the eye of the needle as seen in the conversion of Zacchaeus, a wealthy tax collector (Luke 19:1–10).

Summary

Worldliness, however, is not just reflected in where people go, in what they do, in what their financial status is, or with whom they associate, but worldliness has its roots in a person's heart. John makes it perfectly clear that these three realities (the lust of the flesh, the lust of the eyes, and the boastful pride of life) are not from God but from the world. What hangs in the balance is of eternal importance. To live for the world is to lose everything in the end; the things of the world are transitory, but the one who lives for God lives forever. The choice is clear and the consequences obvious (1 John 2:17).

Being in—but Not of—the World

What hope do believers have against such an alluring system as the seduction of the world? God's Word makes clear that as enticing as the world can be, God has empowered believers to resist the world's seductive attraction. For example, believers have been chosen "from the world" (John 17:6). While they still live in the world of creation and among the world of people, they are no longer captives to the dominion over which Satan rules (John 17:11, 15). Understanding the reality of the world under Satan's dominion explains why the world hates the church (John 15:18–19; 17:14). The world is characterized by hatred, while Christians are to be characterized by love for God (1 John 2:15) and godly love for others (1 John 3:14).

Not Conformed but Transformed

Paul told his readers at Rome, "Do not be conformed to this age, but be transformed by the renewing of your mind" (Rom 12:2). Paul's call to not be conformed to the world's values is a call to not conform to a fallen culture. This call to resist the prevailing age can be heard throughout the Bible. The following are a few examples of such passages:

- "Do not follow the practices of the land of Egypt, where you used to live, or follow the practices of the land of Canaan, where I am bringing you. You must not follow their customs" (Lev 18:3).
- "They rejected his statutes and his covenant he had made with their ancestors and the warnings he had given them. They followed worthless idols and became worthless themselves, following the surrounding nations the Lord had commanded them not to imitate" (2 Kgs 17:15).
- "So you will know that I am the Lord, whose statutes you have not followed and whose ordinances you have not practiced. Instead, you have acted according to the ordinances of the nations around you" (Ezek 11:12).

The world system is always trying to conform God's people into its image. To be conformed into the world's image is to find one's worth in the things of the world; to embrace the world's perspective on honor and shame; to view money, sex, ambition, and pleasure in a manner compatible with worldliness. The world system never rests, and its message rings out continually through media and culture.

Paul urged his readers, instead of being conformed into the image of the world, to "be transformed by the renewing of your mind." This transformation takes place as the Spirit of God uses the Word of God to cause a believer to think more and more in line with Scripture about the things of this world. This transformation ultimately enables believers, whose minds are saturated with Scripture, to discern God's will. John Stott wrote about this transformation:

> These two value systems (this world and God's will) are incompatible, even in direct collision with one another. Whether we are thinking about the purpose of life or the meaning of life, about how to measure greatness or how to respond to evil, about ambition, sex, honesty, money, community, religion or anything else, the two sets of standards diverge so completely that there is no possibility of compromise.[12]

The outworking of this transformation is a Christian mind (cf. Rom 8:1–8): the ability to discern between good and evil, and between the good and the best (Rom 12:2).

---

[12] John R. W. Stott, *Romans: God's Good News for the World*, The Bible Speaks Today (Downers Grove, IL: InterVarsity, 1994), 323–24.

Not the World's Wisdom

As Paul stated in Rom 12:1–2, the true battleground with world-liness is the mind. What a person dwells on determines the choices he or she makes. James made a comparable point:

> Who among you is wise and understanding? By his good conduct he should show that his works are done in the gentleness that comes from wisdom. But if you have bitter envy and selfish ambition in your heart, don't boast and deny the truth. Such wisdom does not come down from above but is earthly, unspiritual, demonic. For where there is envy and selfish ambition, there is disorder and every evil practice. But the wisdom from above is first pure, then peace-loving, gentle, compliant, full of mercy and good fruits, unwavering, without pre-tense. And the fruit of righteousness is sown in peace by those who cultivate peace. (Jas 3:13–18)

James contrasted two kinds of wisdom, one from above and the other from below. One comes from heaven and the other from hell (demonic). The kind of wisdom prevailing in a person's thoughts is evidenced by what comes out of his or her heart in everyday life (Mark 7:20–23; Matt 12:34). Wickedness cannot come out of you unless it is first within you. If a marriage is filled with envy, argumen-tation, bitterness, and continual bickering, then the prevailing wisdom is earthly, unspiritual, and even demonic. The renewing of the mind changes the way people think and results in behavioral changes.[13]

---

[13] For practical help in this area, see Paul David Tripp, *Instruments in the Redeemer's Hands: People in Need of Change Helping People in Need of Change*, Resources for Changing Lives (Phillipsburg, NJ: P&R, 2002).

The revealing of worldly thinking in a home should cause a couple to call out to God. They should search God's Word together for the foundation of a healthy marriage. They should confess their sin to one another. They should seek to order their home according to the teachings of Scripture rather than the pressures of secular society. God is for the family, and his Word helps believers recognize when the world's wisdom is taking hold in their home.

What is true in the family is equally true in the life of a single person. A life filled with turmoil and conflict may be evidence that a person is listening to the wrong voices—following the wrong kind of wisdom. God's wisdom does not necessarily result in an easy life, but it does result in a godly life.

Overcoming Faith

We return to the apostle John, who stated forthrightly, "Everyone who has been born of God conquers the world. This is the victory that has conquered the world: our faith" (1 John 5:4). This does not mean the victory is easy, as the world is attractive to a believer's flesh (see the next chapter). If faith is the victory that overcomes the world, what can believers do to grow in their faith?

Christians often think of faith in static terms, but faith should be thought of more in dynamic terms. How can faith grow, mature, and develop? First, we must read and know the Word. Paul taught, "So faith comes from what is heard, and what is heard comes through the message about Christ" (Rom 10:17). Whether in the baby stage or a more mature stage of a believer's life, regular reading and study of the Bible strengthen a believer's faith. As we mentioned earlier, the Spirit of God uses the Word of God in the people of God to conform them into the image of the Son of God. Never underestimate the importance of reading the Bible consistently for the development of faith.

A second way for a believer's faith to grow is to ask God to increase their faith. As James stated, "You do not have because you do not ask" (Jas 4:2). Jesus encountered a man who did this very thing, "I do believe; help my unbelief!" (Mark 9:24). Everyone can relate to this father's plea for greater faith. Pray passionately and consistently for greater faith. The author of Hebrews said, "without faith it is impossible to please God" (Heb 11:6).

A third recommendation for growing in our faith to overcome the world is to exercise faith. If we ask God to increase our faith, then God will put us in circumstances where we must exercise our faith. Faith can be compared to a muscle. The more a muscle is used and exercised, the stronger the muscle becomes. But if one does not exercise one's muscles, when that muscle is needed it will be too weak to perform the desired task. The same can be said of faith. For faith in God to be strong, it must grow, mature, and be exercised. For example, Paul commends prayer in Phil 4:6–7 in a manner that suggests both that prayer is an exercise of faith and will result in peace (the opposite of being anxious).

The Church and the World

Unfortunately, the world is having a significant impact on churches. The evidence is that churches are taking their cues more from culture than God's Word. Pragmatism is more important than truth, and church-as-business is more prominent than church as God's called-out people. Numbers, buildings, and

budgets, rather than faithfulness to God's Word, are the deter-
minative factors of "success." As noted earlier in this book, some
worship services are geared more toward entertaining than leading people in the worship of the one true and living God. People
are clamoring for shorter and shorter sermons, and those in the
pulpits are accommodating them.

Seldom do church leaders jump immediately on the band-
wagon of "nickels and noses" as the measure of success. But the
onslaught of podcasts, books, and seminars by so-called evangelical superstars encouraging corporate approaches to leadership
rather than washing feet and leading as God's under-shepherds
can wear down one's resolve to biblical fidelity. Church health
must still trump church growth.

We do well to remember 1 Cor 3:6, "[Paul] planted, Apollos
watered, but God gave the growth." If this was true with the
greatest missionary and church planter in history, then it is true
for your church and ministry as well. Church health and church
growth, of course, are not necessarily mutually exclusive. Many
large churches are faithful to God's Word and resist the "nickel
and nose" approach to ministry. Our point is that church leaders
must pay special attention to their motives and methods. They
must make sure their guidebook is God's Word and not corporate America.

Conclusion

Despite all that has been said about worldliness, Jesus wants his
followers to be *in* the world evangelistically but not *of* the world
morally (John 17:14–17). One's initial inclination after reading
about the danger of worldliness may be to withdraw from the

world of people, to isolate oneself, and to have as little to do with non-Christian people as possible. A well-intended believer may get rid of the television, turn off his or her podcasts, cancel his or her internet, and cease participating in community activities. While these are admirable ways to apply Jesus's exhortation to take serious measures against sin, complete and prolonged withdrawal from society is to miss the point.

Jesus left heaven to enter the world that he might redeem a people for God. He entrusts those whom he saves with the good news and sends them out into the world. Jesus calls them to holiness and nonconformity, not to isolation. Christians are called to be salt and light. Salt is next to worthless if it remains in the saltshaker. Light is intended to illuminate the darkness, not to be hidden. The Vanity Fair of this world is holding billions of people captive, and the church must love the world of people enough to share their faith, while at the same time "keep[ing] oneself unstained from the world" (Jas 1:27) and rejecting the seduction of this evil age.

CHAPTER 3

Crucify the Flesh

The enemy of every Christian is a three-headed monster—the world, the flesh, and the devil. Two of these assail the believer from without (the world and the devil) and one from within (the flesh). Clinton Arnold defines the flesh as "the inner propensity or inclination to do evil. It is the part of our creatureliness tainted by the fall that remains with us until the day we die. The flesh is our continuing connection to this present evil age, which is destined to perish but against which we must struggle now."[1] Therefore, when used in a theological sense, "the flesh" refers to the fallen, sinful, corrupt human nature, which every person inherits from Adam.

The following verses from Galatians and Romans provide a few examples of the term's theological usage:

---

[1] Arnold, *3 Crucial Questions about Spiritual Warfare*, 34 (see chap. 1, n. 2).

- "I say, then, walk by the Spirit and you will certainly not carry out the desire of the flesh. For the flesh desires what is against the Spirit, and the Spirit desires what is against the flesh; these are opposed to each other, so that you don't do what you want" (Gal 5:16–17).
- "Now those who belong to Christ Jesus have crucified the flesh with its passions and desires" (Gal 5:24).
- "Because the one who sows to his flesh will reap destruction from the flesh, but the one who sows to the Spirit will reap eternal life from the Spirit" (Gal 6:8).
- "For those who live according to the flesh have their minds set on the things of the flesh, but those who live according to the Spirit have their minds set on the things of the Spirit" (Rom 8:5).
- "But put on the Lord Jesus Christ, and make no provision for the flesh to gratify its desires" (Rom 13:14).

When one lives "according to the flesh," one makes self-centered, sinful choices that gratify the desires of the flesh. This self-centered way of life is behind much of the wickedness of this present age and can be seen in governmental corruption, corporate greed, internet pornography, the sex trade, the yelling and screaming resonating from many homes, entertainment binge-ing, and on and on.

For believers, the irresistible power of the flesh has been broken. Indwelling sin no longer has absolute power over Christians. Sin is no longer the believer's master (Rom 6:11). Despite all this, the believer's indwelling sin (the flesh) is constantly working to reestablish influence in the Christian's life. While the battle to resist the desires of the flesh may be intense, Christians can resist by the indwelling power of the Spirit.

Crucified Flesh in Galatians

Galatians 5:16–26 is a classic text on the battle between the flesh and the Spirit. Because of this passage's importance, it is quoted in full here:

> I say, then, walk by the Spirit and you will certainly not carry out the desire of the flesh. For the flesh desires what is against the Spirit, and the Spirit desires what is against the flesh; these are opposed to each other, so that you don't do what you want. But if you are led by the Spirit, you are not under the law. Now the works of the flesh are obvious: sexual immorality, moral impurity, promiscuity, idolatry, sorcery, hatreds, strife, jealousy, outbursts of anger, selfish ambitions, dissensions, factions, envy, drunkenness, carousing, and anything similar. I am warning you about these things—as I warned you before—that those who practice such things will not inherit the kingdom of God. But the fruit of the Spirit is love, joy, peace, patience, kindness, goodness, faithfulness, gentleness, and self-control. The law is not against such things. Now those who belong to Christ Jesus have crucified the flesh with its passions and desires. If we live by the Spirit, let us also keep in step with the Spirit. Let us not become conceited, provoking one another, envying one another.

The words "flesh" and "Spirit" dominate the passage. The word "flesh" is used five times in the passage and "Spirit" seven times. Paul describes an intense conflict taking place within the life of every Christian (vv. 16–17). The conflict is the battle for holiness. This conflict is a part of the process of sanctification, whereby a believer is conformed more and more into the image of Jesus. Sanctification is a lifetime process. Sometimes the conflict is greater than at other times, but the conflict is an aspect of every Christian's spiritual experience.

Flesh

Paul personifies the flesh as having longings and desires (Gal 5:24). These longings and desires within the believer are indications of the presence of indwelling sin in the believer's life. These fleshly desires may be aroused by previous sinful habit patterns a person has engaged in, or they may be new variations on old vices. At times, these sinful desires may seem so strong that one may feel unable to resist them (v. 18b).

Paul indicates that the outworking of these sinful desires is obvious (v. 19). Paul's catalog of the "works of the flesh" are a horrible picture of godless living, and the list is not exhaustive (v. 21, "and anything similar"). John Stott provides a helpful breakdown of this catalogue of sins.[2] The first three words reference sexual sin, the next two are sins of false religion, the next eight are sins of a social nature, and the last two are associated with drunkenness.

Many believers have read this catalogue of sins and wondered if they are genuinely saved. Paul made a helpful comment at this point: "Those who *practice* such things will not inherit the kingdom of God" (v. 21, italics added). The key thought is found in the word "practice," which suggests habitually engaging in an activity. God's judgment comes on those who practice, or habitually engage in, the sins of the flesh. Those who practice these sins

---

[2] John R. W. Stott, *The Message of Galatians*, The Bible Speaks Today (Downers Grove, IL: InterVarsity, 1968), 147.

and experience no godly remorse or conviction of the Holy Spirit will incur God's judgment.

Paul is not implying some form of Christian perfectionism. Rather, a person who habitually and intentionally engages in sinful behavior without remorse or conviction of sin may very well not be a genuine Christian. Believers continue to battle sin throughout their lives. Christians experience the Holy Spirit's work of conviction and discipline when they know the remorse and disappointment of sinning against their Savior. The thought is not that believers never commit a work of the flesh, but when they do, they are convicted by the Holy Spirit.

Holy Spirit

How can a believer resist these strong inward yearnings to sin against the Lord? The repeated references to the Holy Spirit in the passage remind believers they do not fight the flesh in their own strength. Remember that seeking to have and relying on individual autonomy was what happened in the Fall![3] Instead, believers must live in dependence on the Lord; we must "walk by the Spirit," "be led by the Spirit," "live by the Spirit," and "keep in step with the Spirit" (Gal 5:16, 18, 25, 25). Later, in chapter 6, we will explore more fully the role of the Spirit in the battle against the world, the flesh, and the devil.

The Holy Spirit's presence in the believer's life, however, does not mean the believer can "let go and let God."[4] The Holy Spirit

---

[3] See chapter 1 of this work.

[4] See esp. Andrew David Naselli, *No Quick Fix: Where Higher Life Theology Came From, What It Is, and Why It's Harmful* (Bellingham, WA: Lexham, 2017).

empowers the believer to "crucif[y] the flesh with its passions and desires." Earlier in this passage, Paul used the imagery of warfare to depict the battle between the flesh and the Spirit, and in Gal 5:24 he uses the imagery of crucifixion. Whether the believer engages in combat or crucifixion with the flesh, Christians must remember they have a role to play in their sanctification.

Crucify

What does it mean for a believer to crucify the flesh? Timothy George understands the phrase to communicate the basic demand of Christian discipleship, corresponding to Jesus's call to take up the cross daily and follow him (Luke 9:23). George goes on to state, "The mortifying work of self-crucifixion is a continuous, lifelong process, for this side of heaven we dwell in mortal bodies and are bound by inordinate desires."[5] We understand the concept here to be similar to Paul's language in Rom 8:13, "put to death the deeds of the body."

The language of crucifixion would stir brutal images in the minds of the original readers. Many of them likely witnessed the horrible act of crucifixion. John Stott uses the ancient practice as an analogy to the thought of the crucifixion of the flesh.[6]

---

[5] Timothy George, *Galatians*, New American Commentary (Nashville: B&H, 1994), 524. Hendriksen understands the phrase as a call to "Be in practice what you are (have confessed to be) in principle!" William W. Hendriksen, *Galatians and Ephesians*, New Testament Commentary (Grand Rapids: Baker, 1968), 228. Contra Thomas R. Schreiner, *Galatians*, Zondervan Exegetical Commentary on the New Testament (Grand Rapids: Zondervan, 2010), 351.

[6] Stott, *The Message of Galatians*, 147–48.

While Stott acknowledges that analogies have a way of breaking down at various points, the imagery of crucifixion remains helpful. Ancient criminals condemned to crucifixion normally had committed heinous acts of violence. In an analogous manner, Christians must understand their sin against God as an act of rebellion. To crucify the flesh is to recognize that no sin is a trivial matter.

Christ had to suffer and die to pay the penalty for the sins of his sheep. The ancient practice of crucifixion was indescribably painful. In a similar manner, the crucifixion of the flesh is a painful process also. For example, rejecting a sinful habit is not an easy task. If a believer struggles with gossip, the process of dealing with that gossip will be painful. What might the crucifixion of the sin of gossip involve? First, one must *acknowledge* to the Lord the sinfulness of gossip. Second, one must *recognize* that not only is gossip a sin against God, but it is also a sin against the person with whom the information is shared and the one gossiped about. Third, such a sin requires one to *ask for forgiveness* from God and both the person with whom the gossip was shared and the person gossiped about, if appropriate.

An inappropriate confession may sound like this, "I apologize for telling others you have a big mouth." That kind of confession is not a genuine confession of sin because the blame is placed on the one that was gossiped about. The confession of sin must be sincere without casting blame on the other person. While crucifying the sin of gossip is humbling, it honors God and will eventually result in more Christlike living. As the sin of gossip weakens in a person's life, he or she will find the practice of crucifying the sin easier by refusing to talk about others.

Crucified criminals in the ancient world did not normally die immediately but might languish for a time. The more physically robust the individual, the longer he would fight to live. By analogy, the same is true with sin. The stronger the sin in a person's life, the longer the sin will fight to survive.

Another example of crucifying the flesh is the sin of greed. To crucify the sin of greed can be agonizing to one who has allowed greed to build a stronghold in one's life. When a Christian takes Jesus's words seriously, "It is more blessed to give than to receive," an inner battle will ensue (Acts 20:35). Generosity does not come naturally to most people. Greed, however, does.

What would crucifying the sin of greed look like in a Christian's life? First, believers must confess their greed to God and receive his forgiveness (1 John 1:9). Second, they must ask God to empower them to battle greed. Third, they should examine closely their finances to see where they are spending their money. Fourth, they can make specific changes to their spending habits and find ways to demonstrate generosity.

Greed often results in significant amounts of debt. If a person has accumulated significant debt, that debt must be paid. An attack against greed does not mean one does not pay one's bills, provide for one's family, or take vacations. Crucifying greed means that if someone else looked at our financial records, he or she would consider us to be generous people. Generosity is not determined by the amount one gives, but the sacrifice involved in giving. This understanding of generosity can be found in Mark 12:41–44. The passage reads:

> Sitting across from the temple treasury, he watched how the crowd dropped money into the treasury. Many rich people were putting in large sums. Then a poor widow

came and dropped in two tiny coins worth very little. Summoning his disciples, he said to them, "Truly I tell you, this poor widow has put more into the treasury than all the others. For they all gave out of their surplus, but she out of her poverty has put in everything she had—all she had to live on."

As Jesus sat in the Court of the Women, he saw many wealthy people putting large sums of money into the temple treasury. Jesus was not impressed by their large offerings. However, he was impressed by the meager offering of an unnamed widow. Jesus used the opportunity as a teachable moment for his disciples. The widow's offering represented genuine sacrifice. The wealthy gave out of their surplus, but their giving did not involve any sacrifice. By contrast, the widow's offering demonstrated great faith and devotion.

God's measurement of generosity looks different than our measurement. As mentioned above, God considers the amount of sacrifice involved in giving and not simply the amount given (see 2 Cor 8–9). The process of crucifying sin may be a long and arduous battle, but God is glorified, and obedience and victory will come.

Union with Christ

Paul's teaching on the believer's union with Christ is essential to walking in obedience to God.[7] To that important topic we now turn as we consider our need to put sin to death.

---

[7] Campbell has written a very thorough recent work on this topic in Paul. Constantine R. Campbell, *Paul and Union with Christ: An Exegetical and Theological Study* (Grand Rapids: Zondervan, 2012).

Romans 6:1–14 is an important passage on this topic. The believer's union with Christ is illustrated in believer's baptism. As a result of the believer's union with Christ, he or she is dead to sin *and* alive to God. The act of baptism pictures the Christian as dead and buried with Christ (submerged in a watery grave) and resurrected to newness of life (raised out of the water). Romans 6:11 is a succinct summary of these two lines of thought: "So, you too consider yourselves dead to sin and alive to God in Christ Jesus."

A believer's death to sin does not mean that sin (the flesh) has been eradicated in the believer, or that one can live a sinless life. But "death to sin" does mean that the power of sin in the believer's life has been broken. As believers come to understand the reality of their union with Christ, they are empowered to say no to sin and yes to God.

Paul approached the reality of the believer's union with Christ in a slightly different way in Rom 8:5–9. The passage reads:

> For those who live according to the flesh have their minds set on the things of the flesh, but those who live according to the Spirit have their minds set on the things of the Spirit. Now the mindset of the flesh is death, but the mindset of the Spirit is life and peace. The mindset of the flesh is hostile to God because it does not submit to God's law. Indeed, it is unable to do so. Those who are in the flesh cannot please God. You, however, are not in the flesh, but in the Spirit, if indeed the Spirit of God lives in you. If anyone does not have the Spirit of Christ, he does not belong to him.

Paul's thought in these verses is that every person is either "in the flesh" (unregenerate) or "in the Spirit" (a Christian); there is no middle ground. Furthermore, the Christian life should be characterized by victory over the flesh (indwelling sin). The fourfold contrast between living according to the flesh and living according to the Spirit is illustrated here:

after the flesh (vv. 4–5)	after the Spirit (vv. 4–5)
the things of the flesh (v. 5)	the things of the Spirit (v. 5)
the mind of the flesh (vv. 6–7)	the mind of the Spirit (v. 6)
in the flesh (vv. 8–9)	in the Spirit (v. 9)

These are the only two categories of people. People live according to the flesh or according to the Spirit. Everyone is saved or lost, regenerate or unregenerate, headed to heaven or to hell.

People's spiritual condition ("after the flesh" or "after the Spirit") determines the way they think about life. Those "after the flesh" fill their minds with fleshly ambitions, and long to satisfy their fleshly desires. Those who are "after the Sprit" have minds that are in the process of being renewed and are focused more and more on what is honorable, just, pure, lovely, commendable, morally excellent, and praiseworthy (Phil 4:8).

People's thoughts determine their actions, their actions reveal their character, and their character gives evidence of their destiny. Paul stated it this way, "the mind set on the flesh is death, but the mind set on the Spirit is life and peace" (Rom 8:6 NASB). Putting sin to death will not always be easy, but it is certainly possible in Christ.

Sowing and Reaping

Another passage for consideration is Gal 6:8, "the one who sows to his flesh will reap destruction from the flesh, but the one who sows to the Spirit will reap eternal life from the Spirit." Another way of stating this principle is: "We reap what we sow, we reap later than we sow, and we reap more than we sow."[8] The principle of sowing and reaping is true in almost every area of life. If a farmer plants corn, obviously he will not reap apples! A period transpires between the planting of seeds and the harvesting of the crop. When the crop is harvested, the amount harvested supersedes the amount planted.

What is true in farming is equally true regarding one's spiritual life. In general, one has as much of God as one desires. Our relationship to God is as close to God as we want it to be. Stott writes:

> To "sow to the flesh" is to pander to it, to cosset, cuddle and stroke it, instead of crucifying it. The seeds we sow are largely thoughts and deeds. Every time we allow our mind to harbour a grudge, nurse a grievance, entertain an impure fantasy, or wallow in self-pity, we are sowing to the flesh. Every time we linger in bad company whose insidious influence we know we cannot resist, every time we lie in bed when we ought to be up and praying, every time we read pornographic literature, every time we take a risk which stains our self-control, we are sowing, sowing, sowing to the flesh. Some Christians sow to the flesh every day and wonder why they do not reap holiness.[9]

---

[8] I am not certain from whom I first heard this statement; however, I have found it to be immensely helpful.

[9] Stott, *The Message of Galatians*, 170.

Being with Christ

Another way to speak of a believer's union with Christ is the phrase "with Christ." The thought of a believer's being united *with* Christ can be seen in Col 2:20 and 3:1–4:

- "If you died *with Christ* to the elements of this world, why do you live as if you still belonged to the world?" (Col 2:20, italics added).
- "So if you have been raised *with Christ*, seek the things above, where Christ is, seated at the right hand of God. Set your minds on things above, not on earthly things. For you died, and your life is hidden *with Christ* in God. When Christ, who is your life, appears, then you also will appear *with him* in glory" (Col 3:1–4, italics added).

When Paul spoke of being "with Christ," he meant more than merely enjoying Christ's presence. In these two passages, the phrase means believers participate in the four major events of Christ's saving ministry—his death, resurrection, ascension, and return—in such a way that they have experienced the first three events and will one day experience the last. Earlier in our discussion, we noted that baptism depicts the believer's union with Christ in his death (Rom 6:3). Paul makes a similar point in Col 2:20.

The word "death" has a decisiveness about it because people normally think of death as the cessation of life. Death represents the end of a relationship. So, when Paul wrote, "You died with Christ to the elements of this world," he is declaring the direct influence of spiritual powers (demons) has ended. These spiritual powers once had significant sway over the Colossians before their salvation. The only way to be free from their direct influence is to be united with Christ by faith.

In Col 3:1–4, Paul emphasized the believer's resurrection *with* Christ, being seated *with* Christ, and future glory *with* Christ. We as Christians have not only died to the direct influence of supernatural spirits, but we have been raised to an entirely new life. Because of believers' union *with* Christ in these salvific events, we should "seek the things above" and "set [our] minds on things above" (3:1–2). When one seeks the things above, he or she lives for those things that have eternal significance and consequence.

Jesus made a similar statement: "But seek first the kingdom of God and his righteousness, and all these things will be provided for you" (Matt 6:33). To seek the things above means that believers do not live their lives motivated by worldly ambitions and yearning after worldly recognition. The godly qualities enumerated later in the passage are the outworking of seeking the things above. For one to set one's mind on things above does not mean that one does not bother to consider the daily affairs of life. Rather, for one to set one's mind on the things above is to think about all of life from a heavenly and eternal perspective.

Yes, but How?

Paul goes on to explain how seeking the things above and setting one's mind on the things above works its way out in daily living in Col 3:5–15. The passage reads:

> Therefore, put to death what belongs to your earthly nature: sexual immorality, impurity, lust, evil desire, and greed, which is idolatry. Because of these, God's wrath is coming upon the disobedient, and you once walked in these things when you were living in them. But now, put away all the following: anger, wrath, malice, slander,

and filthy language from your mouth. Do not lie to one another, since you have put off the old self with its practices and have put on the new self. You are being renewed in knowledge according to the image of your Creator. In Christ there is not Greek and Jew, circumcision and uncircumcision, barbarian, Scythian, slave and free; but Christ is all and in all.

Therefore, as God's chosen ones, holy and dearly loved, put on compassion, kindness, humility, gentleness, and patience, bearing with one another and forgiving one another if anyone has a grievance against another. Just as the Lord has forgiven you, so you are also to forgive. Above all, put on love, which is the perfect bond of unity. And let the peace of Christ, to which you were also called in one body, rule your hearts. And be thankful.

Out with the Old Self

Since believers have died with Christ, been raised with Christ, and are seated with Christ, they should "put to death" and "put off" the sins of the old life. The doctrinal belief of union with Christ should work its way out in practical Christian living—indicatives (things that are true) beget imperatives (things that you do).

The list of sins delineated in these verses falls into two categories: sexual sins and interpersonal sins. The sins of a sexual nature are sexual immorality, impurity, lust, and evil desires. Paul adds greed to the list, which he equates to idolatry (cf. Eph 5:5).

Too often, when people think of idolatry, they think of bowing down before statues and then let themselves off the hook. An idol is anything a person places above God in his or her devotion and love. Here's a litmus test: if you are willing to sin in order to have something, that something sounds like an idol because it is vying for first place in your devotion. People often make idols out of themselves, their family, profession, possessions, or even a ministry. While these may be good things, they are not to be worshiped and certainly should not rival one's devotion to God. While Paul wrote these words to a first-century audience, his words are as relevant today as they were then.

Satan uses people's sinful tendencies to draw them into committing sins of a sexual nature. For this reason, Christians must be on their guard against the devil's seduction toward sexual sins of all kinds. The other sins delineated in the passage are sins expressed in interpersonal relationships: anger, wrath, malice, slander, lying, and filthy language. A lifestyle characterized by these sins is destined for God's wrath. Once again, Paul is not speaking of some sort of Christian perfectionism. He is warning, however, that a person whose life is *characterized* by these sins may not be born again.

In with the New Self

The counterpart to casting off the sins of the old life is putting on qualities that reflect a person's new life in Christ. The qualities set forth here demonstrate a life transformed by grace: compassion, kindness, humility, gentleness, patience, forbearance, forgiveness, love, peace, and thankfulness. These two lists could not be any more different. Those outside of Christ are characterized by a certain type of behavior. Those who have died with Christ are also characterized by certain behavioral traits.

When Paul says that these qualities are to be put on, he is suggesting that believers have a role to play in their sanctification. Because Christians are dead to sin and alive to God in Christ, they are to put sin to death by the power of the Spirit. To borrow the thought from Gal 5:24, they must crucify the flesh. A godly life is demonstrated by sexual purity.

When devotion to the Lord is your top priority, extreme measures to combat sin are never out of the question. You know this instinctively. If the doctor were to tell you today that he had isolated a strange cancer in one of your limbs and your only course of action to prevent its spread was amputation, your next question would be, "When is the next operating room available?" So, if you recoiled earlier at even the thought of terminating a service that regularly leads to you falling into sin, that ought to be a red flag to you!

Living the Christian life also means treating people in a manner that glorifies God, including speaking kindly to and about others and forgiving those who have wronged us. In these relationships, we show compassion, kindness, humility, gentleness, and patience. None of this comes easy, but because of our union with Christ, it is both expected and possible.

Paul goes on to emphasize the importance of the Word if one is to live a Christ-honoring life. He urges the Colossians to let the Word of Christ dwell in them. The results of the Word richly dwelling in believers is comparable to what Paul says about being filled with the Spirit in Eph 5:18–21. The fullness of the Spirit is closely related to a life saturated by God's Word.

Jesus made a similar point when he told his disciples, "If you abide in me, and my words abide in you, ask whatever you wish, and it will be done for you" (John 15:7 ESV). To abide in the Word "signifies a settled determination to live in the word of

Christ and by it, and so entails a perpetual listening to it, reflection on it, holding fast to it, and carrying out its bidding."[10] A Spirit-filled life is a Word-filled life.

Perhaps another example of how putting sin to death works its way out in a believer's life would be helpful. Anger is a common sin that is easily excused. Paul lists "outbursts of anger" among the deeds of the flesh (Gal 5:20). Over time, anger can gain a foothold in a Christian's life (Eph 5:26–27). Tolerating sinful anger over time desensitizes a person to anger's sinfulness. People often make excuses for their anger, blaming their children, spouses, unfavorable circumstances, their upbringing, or anything else that comes to mind. They no longer realize the devastating damage their anger causes or accept responsibility for their sinful outbursts.

When believers begin to understand that God hates their anger and Jesus had to suffer God's wrath to pay the penalty for their anger, they become serious about killing it. The death of the sin of anger begins with confessing anger as a sin to God. Next, one must ask forgiveness of those who have experienced the brunt of those outbursts of anger. These two steps, however, are just the beginning of the process.

When a sin like anger gains a foothold in a person's life, it will not go away easily. We must pray that the Spirit will make us aware when sinful anger begins to rise within us. We must also recognize that the power of the Spirit is available to counteract that rising hostility. We may even need to leave the room and separate ourselves from the situation causing us frustration.

---

[10] George R. Beasley-Murray, *John*, Word Biblical Commentary 36 (Waco: Word, 1987), 133.

If you face this kind of situation, ask God to calm your heart and give you a clear perspective on what is transpiring. Recognize that sin is knocking at the door and refuse to open the door of your heart to it. You may have no control over your feelings, but you do have control over your mouth and actions. You can use the sword of the Spirit by quoting appropriate verses. You may, in fact, have memorized Eph 4:30–32 in your battle against anger, "And don't grieve God's Holy Spirit. You were sealed by him for the day of redemption. Let all bitterness, anger and wrath, shouting and slander be removed from you, along with all malice. And be kind and compassionate to one another, forgiving one another, just as God also forgave you in Christ."

If you are victorious in that battle with anger, give praise to God. If you sin and express sinful anger, confess it to the Lord and those you sinned against. The battle may be arduous and prolonged, but obedience for God's glory is the goal.

Conclusion

Our goal in the first part of this book has been to remind you about (or introduce you to) the three enemies we face: the devil, the world, and the flesh. If we stop at this point, though, all of us may feel more overwhelmed by the reality and intensity of the battle than hopeful. The story is not over, however.

As Pastor Sam Storms writes, "God has graciously provided for us everything we need to resist and overcome Satan and his demons. In fact, when we employ God's resources and power, we are assured of victory over all Satan's schemes."[11] In the next part, we will look at God's provisions for us to overcome these enemies.

---

[11] Sam Storms, *Understanding Spiritual Warfare* (Grand Rapids: Zondervan, 2021), 298.

PART 2

Knowing God's Provisions

CHAPTER 4

Victory in Temptation

In this second part of the book, our goal is to help you see provisions God offers you to live in victory over the enemy. Those provisions are the Holy Spirit, prayer, and the power to overcome temptation. Because we have just discussed our flesh and indwelling sin, we will begin with the issue of temptation.

Among the titles given to the devil in Scripture, one fits especially well with the subject of this chapter: Tempter (Matt 4:3; 1 Thess 3:5). While not all temptation is directly attributed to the devil's agency in Scripture, the most famous temptation—the temptation of Jesus—is. This story and others will teach us much about living in victory over the enemy.

Jesus Tempted in the Wilderness

One of the most famous episodes in the Bible is Jesus's wilderness temptation.[1] The event is recounted in the Synoptic Gospels (Matt 4:1–11; Mark 1:12–13; Luke 4:1–13). After the Spirit descended on Jesus at his baptism, the Spirit led him into the wilderness to encounter Satan. Mark's account is the briefest, while Matthew and Luke's are longer and very similar. We will examine Luke's account more closely since it has some unique features not found in Mark and Matthew's Gospels.

Adam and Jesus

Jesus's wilderness temptation has similarities to Adam's temptation in the garden. Luke makes a specific connection to Adam by his placement of Jesus's genealogy just before the temptation narrative. Luke's genealogy of Jesus concludes with a reference to Adam as the "son of God," while Satan twice referred to Jesus as the "Son of God" in the temptation narrative (3:38; 4:3, 9).

However, the differences between Adam and Jesus's responses to Satan's temptation could not have been any greater. Adam was tempted in the beautiful Garden of Eden, while Jesus was tempted in the barren Judean wilderness. While Adam could eat from any tree in the garden but one, Jesus ate nothing for forty days. Adam and Eve capitulated and sinned when the snake enticed them, but Jesus resisted the devil's temptations. Jesus, the second and greater Adam, was victorious over the devil in the wilderness.

---

[1] This section is a summary of my discussion in Cook and Lawless, *Spiritual Warfare in the Storyline of Scripture*, 43–50 (see intro., n. 1).

Jesus and Israel

Jesus is not only contrasted with the first Adam in Luke, but also with the nation of Israel.[2] The number forty is significant. Jesus fasted for forty days, while Israel wandered in the wilderness for forty years. Both Jesus and Israel are called God's son (Exod 4:22–23; Deut 8:5). This connection is made more evident by Jesus's three quotations from Deuteronomy 6–8. The three quotes appear in Old Testament contexts where the nation of Israel sinned against God during her wilderness wandering. Where God's son Israel failed in the wilderness, Jesus, the obedient Son, overcame in the wilderness.

The devil's first temptation was an attempt to get Jesus to satisfy his hunger by acting independently from his heavenly Father (Luke 4:3). The devil's words, "If you are the Son of God," should not be understood to be an attempt to get Jesus to doubt his sonship. God had declared Jesus to be his "beloved Son" at his baptism (Luke 3:22). Since Jesus is God's Son, he should have the prerogative to act independently of his Father and meet his own needs. Jesus's response was swift and direct, "Man must

---

[2] David Bauer writes, "The background of this passage is Deuteronomy 6–8, which describes the people of Israel being tempted for forty years in the wilderness and yielding to that temptation. For one thing, the introductory statement that Jesus was led by the Spirit into the desert (or wilderness) to be tempted by the devil alludes to Deuteronomy 8:2. For another thing, three times Jesus responds to temptation with a quote from a passage within Deuteronomy 6–8. Jesus thus relives the experience of Israel in the wilderness but makes good where Israel failed: as Israel God's son was tempted in the wilderness and yielded to this temptation (cf. Deut 8:5), even so Jesus God's Son is tempted in the wilderness but refuses to yield, remaining completely obedient to the will of his Father." David R. Bauer, *The Gospel of the Son of God: An Introduction to Matthew* (Downers Grove, IL: InterVarsity Academic, 2019), 158.

not live on bread alone but on every word that comes from the mouth of God" (Matt 4:4, citing Deut 8:3).

Israel complained to God about God's provision of food in the wilderness. Where Israel sinned, Jesus obeyed. Jesus did not use his supernatural powers to meet his own needs. Complaining is often thought of as an *acceptable* sin. Yet God punished Israel for her complaining. The sin of complaining is an assault against the goodness and providence of God in our lives. Paul said, "Do everything without grumbling and arguing" (Phil 2:14). God takes our complaining much more seriously than we do.

The second temptation in Luke took place on a high mountain. If Jesus would worship the devil, the devil would give him all the kingdoms of the world. This was a satanic attempt to get Jesus to take a shortcut to the establishment of a kingdom. One wonders if the devil had not made a promise he could not possibly keep. The Old Testament makes it perfectly clear that God limits the devil's authority (Dan 4:32; cf. Job 1:6–12). The devil's offer was no more than a half-truth. Jesus quoted again from Deuteronomy (6:13). While Israel was prone to chase after false gods (Exod 32:7–8), Jesus would worship and serve God alone (Luke 4:8). Jesus joins together what people often separate—worship and service. People will serve whatever or whomever they worship.

In the third temptation, Satan quoted Scripture to tempt Jesus to jump from "the pinnacle of the temple" (4:9). The devil quoted Ps 91:11–12, ripping it from its contextual meaning. He tempted Jesus to test God. The circumstance, however, was satanically contrived. If Jesus had jumped from the pinnacle of the temple, he would have been presuming on God's protection. In response, Jesus quoted Deut 6:16. Israel, on the other hand, often tried and tested God's patience in the wilderness (Exod 17:1–7). Where Israel sinned against God, Jesus obeyed.

Learning from Jesus

Jesus's battle with the devil in the wilderness has much to teach us on the matter of resisting temptation. First, Jesus did not leverage his divinity for provision, power, and protection. Jesus not only rejected the devil's temptations but also depended directly upon his Father's word. As Paul put it, "who, existing in the form of God, did not consider equality with God as something to be *exploited*" (Phil 2:6, italics added). Jesus wielded the same sword of the Spirit that God has provided us.

Second, Jesus entered the wilderness "full of the Holy Spirit" (Luke 4:1). Some believers mistakenly think that the more like Christ they become, the less they will be tempted. To this we may make two observations: (1) becoming more Christlike will make us more aware of temptation, and (2) temptation becomes more subtle. Our awareness of temptation increases as we are weaned off the world and satisfied in Christ. As anyone who has attempted to eat clean for an extended period knows, the moment you have any greasy or sugary food, your body knows and revolts. Whereas before you could enjoy fried food or rich fudge whenever you wanted, having cleansed your palate and your body you are now more aware, more sensitive, and more disinclined toward these. The same is true of temptation for the Christian.

Regarding the subtlety of temptation, recall that Adam and Eve were tempted to eat fruit from a forbidden tree, seemingly harmless, but their sinful choice resulted in devastating consequences. Jesus was tempted to satisfy a God-given desire for food by turning a stone into bread, again seemingly harmless. Yet, if Jesus had succumbed to the temptation, he could not have been mankind's Savior. As we strive to become like Christ, we need to be aware of temptations that seem to be innocuous.

Third, Jesus came *out of* the wilderness in "the power of the Spirit" (4:14). Jesus entered the wilderness "full of the Spirit" and departs in "the power of the Spirit." While one must be cautious not to make too much out of this, it does seem Luke intended to make a point. Fullness of the Spirit is for living (Eph 5:18–20), while the power of the Spirit is for ministry. After Jesus returned from the wilderness, he immediately launched into his great Galilean ministry (Luke 4:16–31). Ministry that lacks the Spirit's anointing and power can be the result of a compromised servant.

Fourth, while Satan misused Scripture, Jesus quoted it faithfully in response to each temptation. Jesus knew how to appropriate each passage to combat temptation. In Ephesians, Paul compares Scripture to a sword (Eph 6:17). Jesus showed his people how to wield the "sword of the Spirit." God's Word understood, believed, and obeyed is powerful. The Psalmist asked the question, "How can a young man keep his way pure? By keeping your word" (Ps 119:9). Jesus did not use his supernatural powers to defeat the devil in the wilderness, but God's holy Word—understood, believed, and obeyed. This is the same Word available to every believer in their battle against the spiritual forces of darkness.

Allow us to illustrate one way the devil may work such temptation in your life (a way we do not often consider). C. S. Lewis in his book *Screwtape Letters* envisions a correspondence between two demons, one a master tempter (Screwtape), the other a novice (Wormwood). In one letter Screwtape teaches Wormwood how to subtly subvert a person's allegiance to God (whom Screwtape calls "the enemy") through the fallacious idea of human ownership—that is, through the wrong idea that we somehow "own" ourselves, our time, and everything we have. Listen to Screwtape's words to Wormwood:

> The sense of ownership in general is always to be encouraged. The humans are always putting up claims to ownership which sounds equally funny in Heaven and in Hell, and we must keep them doing so. . . . It is as if a royal child whom his father has placed, for love's sake, in ritual command of some great province, under the real rule of wise counsellors, should come to fancy he really owns the cities, the forest, and the corn, in the same way as he owns the bricks on the nursery floor. . . . We have taught [people] to say "my God" in a sense not really very different from "my boots," meaning "the God in whom I have a claim for my distinguished services and whom I exploit from the pulpit—the God I have done a corner in." And all the time the joke is that the word "Mine" in its fully possessive sense cannot be uttered by a human being about anything.[3]

Paul, on the other hand, reminded us, "You are not your own, for you were bought at a price" (1 Cor 6:19–20). When we think everything is ours (or "mine"), we have bought into one of the enemy's lies. We make ourselves the master—and that's idolatry.

Jesus's wilderness temptation provides us a model for defeating the devil. In this life, temptation is certain, but thanks to

---

[3] C. S. Lewis, *The Screwtape Letters with Screwtape Proposes a Toast* (New York: Macmillan, 1961/1998), 97–98.

Jesus's example, the Spirit's indwelling, and God's Word, victory over the enemy is possible.

Anatomy of a Temptation

Unraveling the individual roles of Satan, indwelling sin, and the world is not an easy task. James 1:13–16, however, focuses the spotlight on an individual person's fallen desires as a source of temptation.

Context of James 1

The context of this passage is essential for grasping fully James's intended meaning in vv. 13–16. James instructed his readers in vv. 3–12 on the topic of life's trials. The words "temptation" and "trial" translate the same Greek word. The context determines the way the word is to be translated.

James encouraged his readers to "count it all joy" (v. 2 ASV) when they encounter various trials because God uses these trials in the lives of his people for spiritual maturity (vv. 3, 12). This does not mean that trials are pleasant. They most certainly are not, but it does mean that God plans to use them in his people's lives to mature them spiritually.

It may be helpful to unpack vv. 2–4 to better understand how trials and temptation differ. Life is filled with all sorts of trials. Some of them are more like pop quizzes and others major exams. Whether it is the loss of a job or the loss of a loved one, we all encounter testing. We do not, though, always respond the same way.

Indeed, people respond in a variety of ways to life's tests. Some people respond with denial—"this is not happening to me"—and they go on as if nothing's happening. Others look for ways to escape—drugs, one-night stands, excessive spending, entertainment bingeing, overeating. Sometimes we blame ourselves when we are facing testing, while others look around for someone else to blame. James wants believers to understand that God uses life's testing to mature believers in their faith. God never wastes our sorrows, nor should we.

James made it clear by his use of the word "when" (v. 2 ASV) that testing will come. He did not say *if*, but *when*. There is no way to avoid testing in this fallen world. Sickness and heartache come to the godliest of people. Trials are the consequences of living in a fallen world. Trials are a reminder that we are not home yet.

James wrote of "encounter[ing] various trials" (NASB). The word translated "encounter" here is used also in the parable of the good Samaritan (Luke 10:30 NASB). In that passage, a man "encountered" robbers. The idea is he unexpectedly fell in among a group of thieves and was beaten and left for dead. That is what it often feels like when life's tests "jump" us. These unexpected and surprising trials can come out of nowhere.

The word "various" communicates the multicolored nature of trials; trials come monogrammed with our initials. The proper response to these testing times, then, is to respond to them with "great joy" (v. 2)—a response that sounds counterintuitive! Rejoicing in our trials may not come naturally, but it is a common admonition in the Bible (1 Pet 1:6–7; 4:12–13; Rom 5:3–5).

In v. 3, James equated the trials of v. 2 with "the testing of your faith." Many believers unconsciously believe a form of the health-wealth gospel—"if I do good things, good things will always happen to me." We must remember, however, that we live in a fallen world and bad things happen to good people. God, in fact, uses the crucible of suffering to cause our faith to mature. This is the reason James said, "*knowing* the testing of your faith produces endurance" (NASB, italics added). James encouraged his readers to rejoice because they know God uses trying times to produce endurance leading to spiritual maturity (v. 4).[4] We do not need to go looking for testing times so we can grow spiritually; God allows them to come in his time.

In vv. 5–8, James instructs his readers to make prayer a priority, especially during a trying time. In vv. 9–11, he illustrates that both riches and poverty can have their own sets of trials. Verse 12 is a promise that those who demonstrate their love for the Lord by persevering through trying times will be rewarded (v. 12).

James on Internal Temptation

The previous discussion helps set the context for James's discussion on internal temptation. Believers are to rejoice in their trials, not because they are pleasant, but because God uses them to refine our faith. Temptation, however, must be resisted. "No one undergoing [temptation] . . . should say, 'I am being tempted by God,' since God is not tempted by evil, and he himself doesn't tempt anyone. But each person is tempted when he is drawn away and enticed by his own evil desire. Then after desire has conceived, it gives birth to sin, and when sin is fully grown, it gives birth to death" (Jas 1:13–15). James began by declaring that no one should blame God when he or she is being tempted

---

[4] The participle *ginōskontes* is causal. See Craig L. Blomberg and Mariam J. Kamell, *James*, Zondervan Exegetical Commentary on the New Testament 16 (Grand Rapids: Zondervan, 2008), 49; Moo, *The Letter of James*, 52–55 (see chap. 1, n. 8).

(v. 13). God cannot be tempted because of his perfect holiness, and he does not entice people to sin.

In v. 14, James explained the conception of sin in the human heart. Contrary to "the devil made me do it" theology, temptation to sin comes from elements that have their roots in a person's own heart. The words translated "drawn away" (lured) and "enticed" (ensnared) are taken from the hunting and fishing world. The picture is that of a fish swimming a straight course and being drawn off by a deadly hook. The first term is used in the Greek Old Testament when the men of Israel lured Benjamin out of Gibeah to ambush them (Judg 20:31). The second term is used by Philo, a Greek-speaking Jewish philosopher in the first century, to describe the fall of Adam and Eve: "the mind being immediately *caught by the bait* (*deleasasa*), becomes a subject instead of a ruler, and a slave instead of a master, and an exile instead of a citizen, and a mortal instead of an immortal."[5]

That which lures and then ensnares a person, James said, is, surprisingly, their own lust. James's point is to reject any attempt to shift the blame for wrongdoing from oneself to outward circumstances or inherited tendencies. Later in his epistle, James will insist that "we do what we do because we want what we want" (cf. 4:1–4).[6]

In v. 15, James shifted his imagery to childbearing. He vividly portrayed how lustful desires break out into actual acts of sin.

---

[5] This translation of Philo's *On the Creation*, §165, comes from Philo of Alexandria, *The Works of Philo: Complete and Unabridged*, trans. Charles Duke Yonge (Peabody, MA: Hendrickson, 1995), 23, emphasis added.

[6] This quote is the apt summary of James's language, which is used frequently in counseling contexts by Dr. Brent Aucoin of Faith Church in Lafayette, IN. His lectures on this topic are available at faithlafayette.org /heart (accessed 3/19/2022).

The suggestion is that a person's "lust" is like a harlot who entices and seduces him. A person surrenders his or her will to lust, conception takes place, and lust gives "birth to sin." The conclusion of this process is death—lust, sin, death is the progression. Although a fleeting lustful thought may seem insignificant, if not put to death (Col 3:5), it will beget more of itself (like begets like). If we encountered cockroaches in our kitchen, we would not ignore them (they would multiply!)—we would call the exterminator! So, why would we ever let parasitic lustful thoughts go unchecked?

What about Satan?

James makes no reference to Satan in this discussion of temptation, a silence about which we may make some observations. It was not James's intention to give full discussion of the origin and development of sin, but only to show how enticement to sin cannot come from God. James stresses the inward nature of temptation to divest people of any excuses for their sin. Satan clearly has his part in temptation, to be sure, but James was anxious that no one defend oneself by throwing the blame on any external source. Certainly, God is not to be blamed, and we cannot ultimately throw the blame at the feet of someone else for our sinful choices. As we noted earlier, "we do what we do because we want what we want."

Yet we may not be far afield to understand Satan (or a demon) as the fisher who has baited the hook with the object of our desire. Knowing what a person's sinful inclinations are is not hard to determine. (Just ask a person's spouse; the spouse knows!) How a person responds when he or she sees the enticement of the lure will determine whether that individual takes the "bait." Will one take a second look, push the website button, make an unwise purchase, or allow one's mind to wander to places it should not go? These are the sort of issues that hang in the balance when we catch a glimpse of the bait out of the corner of our eye. This is also when we must turn to God in prayer and to his Word for defensive action, and then resolve by the Spirit's power and for Christ's glory, "I will not go there!"

The battle may be intense, but the stakes are high. The end is death. This recalls the tragic situation in Eden with Adam and Eve. James does not likely mean physical death, though at times that can be a possibility, but instead the death of a relationship, damage to one's communion with Christ and the church. Lust causes one to lose one's spiritual sensibility and make irrational choices. We must guard our mind and heart.

How to Fail to Enter the Promised Land

If you are looking for a road map on how to fall to temptation, look no further than the Exodus generation in the Bible (1 Cor 10:1–13). This seeming change of direction in this chapter may surprise you, and you may not immediately grasp why we're focusing on the Exodus generation in a chapter related to temptation. We go to this story because the final verse in the 1 Corinthians 10 passage is a magnificent promise that God will provide his people a way of escape from temptation (10:13): "No temptation has come upon you except what is common to humanity. But God is faithful; he will not allow you to be tempted beyond what you are able, but with the temptation he will also provide the way out so that you may be able to bear it." The verse, however, like every verse, must be examined within its present context.

The Context of 1 Corinthians 10

The passage itself falls within a larger context. First Corinthians 8:1–11:1 is Paul's discussion on Christian freedom and eating meat offered to idols. While eating meat offered to idols is not often an issue in a Western context, Christian liberty certainly is an important matter. Broadly speaking, Paul encourages his readers to limit their freedom out of love for fellow believers (8:1–13), for gospel advancement (9:1–23), and concern for one's own spiritual well-being (9:24–10:13). The third point is that while some activities may be permissible for believers, that does not mean they are beneficial to their spiritual lives. In 9:24–27, Paul establishes the principle that self-control is essential in the Christian pursuit of holiness if one is to run one's Christian race well.

First Corinthians 10:1–13 is the example of how the Exodus generation did not run their race well. Although they experienced so many blessings and unimaginable privileges, they failed to enter the Promised Land (cf. Heb 3:7–4:11). Paul's main point in this passage is that the possession of rights and privileges does not assure godliness. The Israelites are an example of what happens to those who fail to exercise self-control in their spiritual lives (cf. 1 Cor 9:24–27).

Beware of Depending on Past Spiritual Victories (10:1–6)

Now I do not want you to be unaware, brothers and sisters, that our ancestors were all under the cloud, all passed through the sea, and all were baptized into Moses in the cloud and in the sea. They all ate the same spiritual food, and all drank the same spiritual drink. For they drank from the spiritual rock that followed them, and that rock was Christ. Nevertheless God was not pleased with most of them, since they were struck down in the wilderness.

Now these things took place as examples for us, so that we will not desire evil things as they did. (1 Cor 10:1–6)

In the first six verses of 1 Corinthians 10, Paul delineates five privileges granted to Israel, which did not guarantee subsequent blessings. Note Paul's repeated use of the word "all" in these verses (vv. 1 [2 times], 2, 3, 4). First, they *all* experienced God's guidance by day in the cloud and his protection by night in a pillar of fire (v. 1a). The Exodus generation left Egypt under God's leadership and guidance (Exod 13:21–22). Second, God providentially governed creation for *all* of them to cross the Red Sea on dry ground (v. 1b).[7] When they were hemmed in by the Egyptian army, God parted the waters of the Red Sea to allow an escape (Exod 14:22–29). God then caused the sea to collapse on the Egyptian army and destroyed them completely. One wonders how the Hebrews could have ever failed to trust and obey God after witnessing that event.

Third, *all* the Exodus generation was blessed with the privilege of being under one of the Old Testament's greatest men as their leader (Moses) (v. 2b). Yet they failed so often to listen to him and regularly complained against him (see Num 11–21). The reference to "baptism" here suggests their submission and allegiance to Moses.[8] Fourth, God provided food for *all* the nation

---

[7] For a thorough treatment of God's providence over nature, see Piper, *Providence*, 221–52 (see chap. 1, n. 14).

[8] As Schreiner writes, "There is a sense in which Israel, through the great redemptive event of the exodus, was incorporated into Moses and established as the people of God." Thomas R. Schreiner, *1 Corinthians: An*

in this barren wasteland—manna and quail (v. 3a; Exod 16:4, 35). Yet they were never quite satisfied with God's provision. Fifth, God provided water for them to drink in the wilderness (v. 4). In many ways, these blessings pointed forward to Jesus. God provided for their physical and spiritual sustenance. The rock from which the water came, and the manna, were symbolic of supernatural sustenance through Christ, the Bread of Life (John 6:35) and the source of the Water of Life (John 4:13–14).

Now we can feel the force of the word "nevertheless" that begins v. 5! Despite these tremendous privileges given to Israel, they still failed to trust and obey God (v. 5). Of the adults who came out of Egypt, only Joshua and Caleb entered the Promised Land (Num 14:5–12). Old Testament scholar John Currid points out about Numbers 14 that, ironically, the Israelites who had exclaimed against the Lord in 14:2, "if only we had died in this wilderness," are going to get what they wished for (14:28–30), and their children whom they said, "would become plunder" (14:3, 31), they would actually inherit the Promised Land.[9] If the Exodus generation had trusted the Lord, they could have not only experienced God's promises fulfilled, but also seen their children and grandchildren in the Promised Land.

What can we learn from this passage? Paul made two important points in vv. 6 and 11. First, we should never underestimate the power of indwelling sin: "Now these things took place as examples for us, so that we will not desire evil things as they did" (v. 6). This truth is exactly what we learned from James.

Introduction and Commentary, The Tyndale New Testament Commentaries 7 (Downers Grove, IL: IVP Academic, 2018), 200.

[9] See John D. Currid, *A Study Commentary on Numbers*, EP Study Commentary (Darlington, England: EP Books, 2009), 203–4.

Second, the experience of the Exodus generation should be a warning to the church: "These things happened to them as examples, and they were written for our instruction, on whom the ends of the ages have come" (v. 11). They fixed their hearts on sinful things and failed to resist the sinful cravings of their fallen nature. Although they participated in some of redemptive history's most significant events, it did not ensure their entry into the Promised Land and result in their spiritual maturity. Past spiritual victories and blessings are not sufficient for future battles. Past godliness can never be an excuse for present disobedience.

Beware of Indications of Spiritual Downfall

In 1 Cor 10:7–11, Paul provided four examples of Israel's unfaithfulness as a call to beware of religious experiences that do not push you to holy living. The passage reads:

> Don't become idolaters as some of them were; as it is written, The people sat down to eat and drink, and got up to party. Let us not commit sexual immorality as some of them did, and in a single day twenty-three thousand people died. Let us not test Christ as some of them did and were destroyed by snakes. And don't grumble as some of them did, and were killed by the destroyer. These things happened to them as examples, and they were written for our instruction, on whom the ends of the ages have come.

As we see in Moses's description of the wilderness wanderings, the Israelites regularly succumbed to the sin of idolatry

(10:7). Idolatry is loving and trusting anyone, or anything more than you love and trust God (Eph 5:5).

Idolatry is rampant in American culture. In secular society, there is an insatiable desire for more money and better bodies, exactly those things the health-wealth gospel promises. How easy it is to follow the idols of money, sex, and power.[10] Our hearts are easily drawn away from a sincere devotion to Jesus.

Paul here refers to the incident of the golden calf in Exodus 32:1–6. Why do people continually turn to idols? Often, they fail to contrast their idols with the greatness of the one true and living God (even though God does this for them in Isa 44:6–46:13). Our idols are man-made, like homes and cars, but God is self-existent. Our contemporary idols provide brief satisfaction, like money and sex, but God provides eternal pleasures (Ps 16:11). Our idols make promises they can't keep, like ultimate satisfaction, but God's promises can be trusted. Our idols are deaf, mute, and heartless, but God hears the prayers of his people and loves his children.

Beale is right that "we become like what we worship."[11] Thus, we are not surprised to see the Lord call his people "you deaf . . . you blind . . . Though seeing many things, you pay no attention. Though his ears are open, he does not listen" (Isa 42:18–20; cf. 6:9–10). They were toward the Lord what their idols were to them: deaf, blind, and unfeeling!

---

[10] See esp. Timothy J. Keller, *Counterfeit Gods: The Empty Promises of Money, Sex, and Power, and the Only Hope That Matters* (New York: Dutton, 2009).

[11] G. K. Beale, *We Become What We Worship: A Biblical Theology of Idolatry* (Downers Grove, IL: InterVarsity Academic, 2008).

The Exodus generation fell into sexual sin (10:8). God has given people a sexual drive to be satisfied within the context of a monogamous marriage between a man and a woman (1 Cor 7:9). Satan tempts people to meet a God-given desire in a God-forbidden manner. Paul refers to Israel joining herself to Baal of Peor and to the men engaging in immorality with Moabite women (Num 25:1–9).

This is why Jesus used the hyperbole that if your eye causes you to sin, then gouge it out. Obviously, he did not mean literally because the issue is the heart, but do not let yourself off the hook with that comment! The point he is making is that we must deal ruthlessly with temptation. We must guard our eyes in what television shows we watch and what content we choose to browse (or we might need to give up that service or stop browsing the internet). What we gaze at captures our hearts. What we give attention to may claim our affection. As we will soon see, this was true of King David and his horrific fall with Bathsheba.

The Exodus generation was guilty of testing God (10:9). When we test God, we are attempting to get him to serve us rather than for us to serve him. To test the Lord is to push him for our own sake. This is similar to what children do when they see how far they can push their parents before their parents will give in to them.

Paul here alluded to Num 21:4–9, where the people grumbled at Moses about life in the wilderness.[12] This is how Satan tempted Jesus in the wilderness: Satan attempted to get Jesus

---

[12] See Naselli, *The Serpent and the Serpent Slayer*, 70–78 (see chap. 1, n. 10).

to do something—jump from the pinnacle of the temple—that God had not led him to do. Jesus had no promise from God that he would protect him if he did that which God had not called him to do. We test God when we put ourselves in compromising situations and then expect God to get us out of them.[13]

Finally, the Exodus generation was guilty of grumbling against God, which is a challenge to God's goodness (10:10). This is probably a reference to Num 16:41–50, when the people rebelled against God's judgment of Korah's rebellion, which led to an additional 14,700 deaths.[14] As we have noted earlier, we often think lightly of grumbling, but it reveals something about our hearts. Jesus said, "The mouth speaks from the overflow of the heart" (Matt 12:34).

---

[13] For this reason, choosing to live in temptation is unwise and ultimately sinful. Consider the following observations: (1) we are tempted by our own desires (Jas 1:14); (2) our heart is deceitful (Jer 17:9) such that our motives may not be clear to us; (3) Jesus counseled his disciples to pray *against* entering temptation (Mark 14:38; Matt 26:41); (4) Jesus taught us to pray with the phrase "lead us not into temptation but deliver us from the Evil One" (Matt 6:13 NIV; cf. Luke 11:4); (5) Jesus pronounced a curse upon those who willingly bring about temptation (Matt 18:7); (6) God provides a way of escape from temptation but never tempts or lures into it (1 Cor 10:13; Jas 1:13); (7) Paul regularly says about sexual temptation not endure but *flee* (1 Cor 6:18; 1 Tim 6:11; 2 Tim 2:22); (8) Paul teaches that sexual immorality and all impurity "must not even be named among you" (Eph 5:3 ESV), which means that we should live in such a way that charges of immorality and impurity could not possibly stick (elsewhere this is called living "above reproach" [1 Tim 3:2; Titus 1:7]). Therefore, choosing to live in temptation puts God to the test and flies in the face of vast swaths of biblical wisdom. As Proverbs 6:27–28 says, "Can a man carry fire next to his chest and his clothes not be burned? Or can one walk on hot coals and his feet not be scorched?" (ESV).

[14] See Schreiner, *1 Corinthians*, 205.

Beware of Rationalizing

Paul did not want his readers to miss the main point of these examples (10:11)—the Exodus generation struggled with the age-old sin of overconfidence (10:12): "whoever thinks he stands must be careful not to fall."[15] We should never think that this could never happen to us. Many godlier people than you and I have slowly succumbed to the continual onslaught of temptation. Giving in a little bit here and a little bit there weakens the foundation of our lives.

This verse is a solemn reminder about the danger of over-confidence. The word "stands" in v. 12 possibly communicates the idea of the precariousness of pride, the "invincible" pride that comes before the fall (Prov 16:18). The fall is a reference to a moral failure or giving in to temptation.

God's Escape Plan

We come now to one of the great promises of the Bible. Verse 13 is the climax of this section: "No temptation has come upon you except what is common to humanity. But God is faithful; he will not allow you to be tempted beyond what you are able, but with the temptation he will also provide the way out so that you may be able to bear it." When you are tempted, look for a way out.

---

[15] We are reminded of the key text from Jonathan Edwards's sermon "Sinners in the Hands of an Angry God" preached on July 8, 1741: "Vengeance belongs to me; I will repay. In time their foot will slip, for their day of disaster is near, and their doom is coming quickly" (Deut 32:35; cf. Ps 73:18). See Jonathan Edwards, "Sinners in the Hands of an Angry God," Blue Letter Bible, accessed September 12, 2022, https://www.blueletterbible.org/study/he_is_risen/jonathan_edwards/sinners.cfm.

God promises to provide you a way of escape (v. 13). Let us think about this verse more closely considering the significant role it plays in this passage and in our battle with temptation.

We live in a culture not unlike that of the Corinthians. Contemporary culture is filled with moral degradation and pressures. Paul's encouragement to the Corinthians is equally encouraging and instructive for twenty-first century Christians. First, the temptations the Corinthians faced were not unique to them, nor are our temptations unique to us. We should not despair by thinking, "No one has ever faced the temptations I'm facing." That kind of thinking is just not true according to Scripture.

The Exodus generation faced temptations to idolatry, sexual promiscuity, testing God's patience by a dissatisfaction with his provisions, and grumbling against God's appointed leaders. The Corinthians were facing these very temptations. The Corinthians' temptations may have been dressed in a slightly different garb, but they were much the same as the Exodus generation. We often think our situations are quite unique, and no one has ever experienced the kind of temptation we are facing. God's Word says that is not true. God's people throughout the ages have resisted similar temptations, and so can you.

Second, any temptation can be resisted because God will help you resist it. Paul states that "God is faithful." Our strength and ability to resist temptation is not based upon our faithfulness to God, but God's faithfulness to us. God's faithfulness is demonstrated by his strengthening us in the face of temptation (2 Cor 12:9; Eph 3:14, 16; 6:10; Phil 4:13; 2 Pet 1:4). God's faithfulness is demonstrated to us by giving us his Word to use as a spiritual sword (Eph 6:17). God's Word renews our minds to provide wisdom from above to make wise choices when tempted (Rom 12:1–2; Jas 3:17). God's faithfulness is demonstrated by his reminder that sometimes the best defense against temptation is to physically remove yourself from the temptation (2 Tim 2:22). Leon Morris observes that the imagery is that of an army trapped in the mountains, which escapes from a seemingly impossible situation through a pass.[16] David's sin with Bathsheba is an example of one who failed to take God's escape route, and the consequences were devastating. As we have mentioned, a moral fall does not typically happen all at once, but a little at a time. But, once it begins, it is hard to reverse because of the momentum we have allowed it to accumulate in our lives. It is like slowly running down a steep hill only to discover that we are picking up more and more speed and cannot stop. Eventually we fall and begin to roll down the hill, or we run into a tree!

This can be seen in the fall of King David. In 2 Samuel 11, David falls into temptation, sinking deeper and deeper into sin. At one time, David was known as a man after God's own heart (1 Sam 13:14). David's demise is set forth in stunning fashion. First, when he should have been leading his troops into battle as their military leader, he stayed behind (11:1).

Second, it is unclear if David was caught off guard by seeing Bathsheba bathing from his rooftop. Regardless, he should have immediately turned away. Unfortunately, his heart was already drifting from God as evidenced by his lingering stare (11:3). The

---

[16] Leon Morris, *1 Corinthians: An Introduction and Commentaries*, Tyndale New Testament Commentary (Revised Edition) (Downers Grove, IL: InterVarsity Press, 1993), 142.

psalmist of Israel had become little more than a perverted person in that moment.

Third, he sinned deliberately and then tried to cover up his sin by deceiving others (11:4–15). Fourth, to protect his "reputation" his sin carried him even further from God into the darkness by the deliberate act of murder (11:15, 17).

Eventually David's sin was exposed by Nathan and punished (12:9–14). By God's grace, he confessed and repented of his sin, and God forgave him. The consequences of David's sin, however, were far-reaching and lasted throughout the remainder of his life.

Believers will be tempted, yet the circumstances that tempt us or test us are no different from those experienced by God's people in every era. As stated above, God is faithful (1 Cor 10:13) and can be trusted to provide a way of escape for those who want it. Sometimes that escape is to turn and run (Joseph, Gen 39:12), and at other times it is to leave the porch, go back into the house, and close the curtains. Never is it to rationalize sinful choices.

Conclusion

Often the major problem in one's battle with temptation is spiritual complacency, a satisfaction with one's walk with Jesus without a sense of needing to go further in discipleship. A. W. Tozer writes in *The Pursuit of God*:

> I want deliberately to encourage this mighty longing for God. The lack of it has brought us to our present low estate. The stiff and wooden quality about our religious lives is a result of our lack of holy desire. Complacency is a deadly foe of all spiritual growth. Acute desire must be present or there will be no manifestation of Christ to

His people. He wants to be wanted. Too bad that with many of us, He waits so long, so very long in vain.[17]

Here are some diagnostic questions for you to ask yourself and meditate on as you finish this chapter: (1) Am I basing my spiritual maturity and reputation in my past victories? (2) Do I give evidence of present victories and blessings in my life? (3) Are there indications that I have cracks in my spiritual foundation? (4) Is there an area in my life where I am not taking advantage of God's escape route by continually giving in to temptation and making excuses? Answer these questions honestly if you want to live in victory over the enemy.

---

[17] A. W. Tozer, *The Pursuit of God* (Chicago: Moody, 1948, 2006), 23.

CHAPTER 5

The Power of Prayer

For many of us, prayer is our last hope rather than our first choice. When prayer is our last option, it is like throwing a Hail Mary pass on the final play of a football game. Hail Mary passes seldom work. Our enemy the devil is always at work, and we must fortify ourselves against his attacks by the Word of God and prayer. A vibrant personal prayer life is essential for victory over the enemy.

A healthy prayer life involves both praying for ourselves and our spiritual needs as well as interceding on behalf of others. In many ways, this chapter is laying the groundwork for what we discuss in chapter 10. What we hope to accomplish in this chapter (and which we expand on later) is the importance of prayer, especially intercessory prayer. In this chapter, we examine not only how important prayer was in Jesus's earthly life, but also how important intercessory prayers were for Paul. We often think of spiritual warfare as relating only to ourselves, but we learn from Paul that spiritual warfare involves fighting alongside others.

We should first think of Jesus. In the Upper Room, Jesus said, "Simon, Simon, look out. Satan has asked to sift you like wheat. But I have prayed for you that your faith may not fail. And you, when you have turned back, strengthen your brothers" (Luke 22:31–32). Simon Peter did fail, but Jesus kept his hand on him, drew him back, and used him to preach the gospel to Jerusalem in Acts 2. One wonders, though, what would have happened to Simon and the other disciples if Jesus had not prayed for them.

Prayer Both Wields and Dons

The importance of prayer as a spiritual assault against the enemy can be seen in Paul's comments in Eph 6:18–20, which come at the end of the most important passage in the Bible on spiritual warfare (Eph 6:10–20).[1] Structurally, Harold Hoehner observes, we must notice that after Ephesians 1–3, Paul has repeatedly used the phrase "therefore . . . walk" to apply the doctrine of the beginning of the letter to his audience (4:1, 17; 5:1–2, 7–8, 15); however, in 6:10 (the last major section of the letter), Paul breaks this pattern with "*Finally*, be strengthened by the Lord" (6:10, emphasis added).[2] This change suggests that just as the same walk (i.e., your intentionally living your life) is in view in each of the five prior instances, so being strengthened in the Lord to

---

[1] Elsewhere, I have discussed the significance of each piece of the armor. Cook and Lawless, *Spiritual Warfare in the Storyline of Scripture*, 145–50 (see intro., n. 1). This discussion is simply homing in on prayer.

[2] Harold W. Hoehner, *Ephesians: An Exegetical Commentary* (Grand Rapids: Baker, 2002), 817.

stand firm against the devil describes the same walk.[3] Spiritual
warfare is not, therefore, something only prayer warriors and pastors are involved in—it is another way of describing your life as
a Christian.

Although Paul's comments about prayer come at the end of
his discussion, we should not presume its placement reflects a
lack of importance. An examination of Eph 6:18–20 will help us
understand more fully Paul's intention.

> Pray at all times in the Spirit with every prayer and
> request, and stay alert with all perseverance and interces-
> sion for all the saints. Pray also for me, that the message
> may be given to me when I open my mouth to make
> known with boldness the mystery of the gospel. For this
> I am an ambassador in chains. Pray that I might be bold
> enough to speak about it as I should.

There are at least three key thoughts to consider in this passage. First, Paul did not compare prayer to a piece of armor or
a weapon as he did other spiritual realities in the passage: belt
(truth), breastplate (righteousness), shoes (gospel of peace),
shield (faith), helmet (salvation), and the sword of the Spirit (the
Word of God). Each of these is ours *in* the Lord—that is, *in*
Christ (truth: 4:21; righteousness: 4:24; gospel: 1:13; faith: 2:5–9;
salvation: 1:13; word: 1:13; 5:26). Rather, prayer is how one takes
up the armor and uses the sword.[4] It is the way that we lean into

---

[3] Jim Rosscup, *An Exposition on Prayer in the Bible: Igniting the Fuel
to Flame Our Communication with God* (Bellingham, WA: Lexham, 2008),
2245.

[4] Cook and Lawless, *Spiritual Warfare in the Storyline of Scripture*,
149; see also Andrew T. Lincoln, *Ephesians*, Word Biblical Commentary
42 (Waco: Word, 2005), 451–52; Ernest Best, *A Critical and Exegetical*

and depend upon the Lord for his strength. As Jim Rosscup puts it, "[Prayer] is the *saturating* element to be crucially at work in every aspect of the armor, to all effective spiritual warfare, and to the whole Christian life."[5]

Second, the repetition of the word "all" underscores the significance of prayer. Believers are exhorted to "pray at *all* times . . . with *all* perseverance and intercession for *all* the saints" (Eph 6:18, italics added). Paul could not have stressed the importance of prayer any more than he does here. The passage drips with urgency.

Third, Paul requests the church at Ephesus to pray for him. Paul knew he needed supernatural empowerment to make gospel inroads. He did not think his own natural abilities sufficient for such a task. If Paul needed prayer, how much more do we, those we love, and other church leaders need prayer?

Considering Paul's words, prayer is one of the most important disciplines a disciple must cultivate for our spiritual growth. Yet, most of us find maintaining a consistent intercessory prayer life difficult. God has given us so many wonderful promises in the Bible to encourage us to pray (Matt 7:7–11; John 14:13–14; 15:7; 1 John 5:14–15), but we still find it difficult to pray consistently.

Commentary on Ephesians, The International Critical Commentary on the Holy Scriptures of the Old and New Testaments (Edinburgh: T&T Clark International, 1998), 604; Peter T. O'Brien, *The Letter to the Ephesians*, The Pillar New Testament Commentary (Grand Rapids: Eerdmans, 1999), 483–84; contrary to Hoehner (*Ephesians*, 854), who limits the participle (*proseuchomenoi*) to "take" in verse 17. However, his comments are applicable to all the armor taken up: "The manner in which this [taking up] is done is to be in a constant state of prayer and alertness" (854).

[5] Rosscup, *An Exposition on Prayer in the Bible*, 2252, emphasis original. His entire treatment of this passage is worth reading (see 2245–58).

Busy lives make it easier to just do life on our own than to find time to pray. Satan fears praying saints, and consequently, when we fail to prioritize prayer, we play right into his hands.

Satan would rather have us do almost anything other than pray (like trying to solve a problem in our own strength). The devil does not want us interceding for our family, praying for God's spiritual blessings on our friends, or asking God's Spirit to empower our church's evangelistic efforts. Prayer calls upon the Lord and depends upon him as our Mighty Warrior (Isa 42:13; cf. Exod 15:3; Ps 24:8; Isa 40:10; Rev 19:11). If we are to defeat the enemy of our souls, we *must* become people of prayer. As mentioned above, this is why the chapter on prayer in the next part of this book offers multiple practical helps for developing our prayer lives.

Jesus's Prayer Life

To say Jesus was a man committed to prayer is one thing, but it is quite another thing to see him praying in the Scripture. Luke's Gospel more than the other three Gospels focuses on Jesus's prayer life. In Luke, Jesus is described as praying at every important moment in his ministry. A brief survey of the Gospel bears this out.

Only the book of Luke describes Jesus praying at his baptism (3:20–21): "Yet he [Jesus] often withdrew to deserted places and prayed" (5:16). Before Jesus chose the Twelve, he spent an entire night in prayer to God (6:12). The point Luke made is that this is the way leaders are to be chosen. In Acts, Luke described a similar situation when the believers prayed before choosing Matthias to replace Judas (Acts 1:24).

Jesus also prayed before asking the Twelve who they thought he was (Luke 9:18). The implication is that Jesus was praying that the disciples would perceive his identity as Messiah. Indeed, this is the first time in Luke's Gospel his disciples acknowledge his Messiahship. In Matthew's Gospel, Jesus's comment on Peter's confession shows the work of the Father in Peter's understanding: "Blessed are you, Simon son of Jonah, because flesh and blood did not reveal this to you, but my Father in heaven" (Matt 16:17).

About a week after that event, Luke describes Jesus praying on the Mount of Transfiguration (9:29). In Luke 10:21–22, we "hear" Jesus's prayer of praise to the Father. In 11:1, Jesus's disciples asked him to teach them to pray like John the Baptist taught his disciples to pray. Jesus responded by teaching them the "Lord's Prayer" as a model for how to pray (11:1–4). He goes on in the passage to stress the importance of persistence in prayer (11:5–13).

In the Upper Room, Jesus told Peter that Satan demanded permission to sift the disciples like wheat, but Jesus interceded for Peter that his faith would not fail (22:31–32). In the unseen world of spiritual reality, a cosmic war was being fought and Satan was preparing to attack the disciples—especially Peter. Jesus engaged in spiritual battle on behalf of Peter and the other disciples by praying for them.[6]

---

[6] Gathercole points out that this passage in Luke betrays two important points about Jesus's preexistence/transcendence: "(1) Jesus is privy to events similar to those going on in the heavenly council in Job 1–2 and thus has some kind of presence there, and (2) he functions already before Easter as a heavenly intercessor combating Satan." Simon J. Gathercole, *The Preexistent Son: Recovering the Christologies of Matthew, Mark, and Luke*

Likewise, in the garden of Gethsemane, Jesus twice told his disciples to pray in order not to fall into temptation (22:40, 46). In the moments following Jesus's time of prayer in the garden, the disciples succumbed to temptation as they fled into the darkness. Jesus, on the other hand, stood strong in defense of his disciples, his soul fortified through prayer.

Once again, Luke gives his readers insight into what was taking place *behind the scenes*: "But this is your hour—and the dominion of darkness" (22:53). Anyone watching these events unfold would have been able to see only a part of what was transpiring: an angry hostile mob, disciples fleeing, and a resolute Jesus. Behind the scenes, a cosmic battle was raging known only to Jesus. That battle led to the cross, where Jesus's first and last words were prayers (23:34, 43).

The purpose in our brief tour of Jesus's prayer life is so we can sense the impact of Jesus's commitment to prayer. Each reference reinforces the thought that Jesus did not believe he could do life without prayer. Considering Jesus's prayer life, we must realize that we cannot live in victory over the enemy without prayer, and much of our prayer times should be focused on intercession.

Inspired Prayer for the Ephesians

A cursory reading of Paul's letters reveals him to be a man of intercessory prayer. I (Bill) do not want you to think praying for matters concerning ourselves is wrong (quite the contrary), but a significant portion of our prayers should be intercessory—i.e., prayer for others. Paul prayed for his converts and requested they

---

(Grand Rapids: Eerdmans, 2006), 51–52. The passage certainly paints a Job 1–2-like scene, except it is pitting *Jesus* against Satan, not Peter.

pray for him. These prayers are marvelous examples of the kinds of requests we can pray for others. In fact, these prayers come from the heart of God since Paul wrote under the inspiration of the Spirit.

When we find ourselves at a loss for what to pray, we can pray the words of Scripture. In fact, we turn our attention now to two Pauline prayers in Ephesians as examples of how to fight for fellow believers in intercession. These two prayers are especially important because of the hostile setting where the Ephesians lived—a city filled with idolatry and occult activity.

Pray That God Would Reveal Himself

In the letter's opening section, Paul praises God for the richness of his blessings showered upon his people—chosen by the Father (1:3–6), redeemed by the Son (1:7–12), and sealed by the Holy Spirit (1:13–14). Paul then transitions from praise to intercession (1:15–23). Paul's motivation to pray for the Ephesians is twofold: (1) God's purposeful sovereignty is evident (note "for this reason" points backward),[7] and (2) it is evident in their faith in Jesus and their love for all the saints (vv. 15–16).

The heart of Paul's intercession is that God would make himself known to the Ephesians (vv. 17–18a). In a city filled with idolatrous worship and occultic practices, Paul prayed the Ephesians would know God ever more deeply. Just like bank

---

[7] For further on how this prayer is grounded on God's sovereign working in the lives of Paul's audience, see D. A. Carson, *A Call to Spiritual Reformation: Priorities from Paul and His Prayers* (Grand Rapids: Baker, 1992), 164–80.

tellers know the difference between genuine currency and a counterfeit by their constant contact with the genuine, so the best defense against false worship and occultic practices (counterfeit gods) is a deeper understanding of who the true God is.

Rather than praying against evil spirits, Paul made a specific request for the believers' spiritual growth. This request was not ethereal but extremely practical. Paul stated precisely what he wanted God to do on their behalf: "I pray that the God of our Lord Jesus Christ, the glorious Father, would give you the Spirit of wisdom and revelation in the knowledge of him. I pray that the eyes of your heart may be enlightened" (vv. 17–18a). Only the Spirit can reveal to a believer the depths of God's greatness.

Paul went on to pray exactly what he desires the Ephesians to learn about God: the hope of God's calling, the glory of God's inheritance in the saints, and the greatness of God's power towards them (vv. 18b–23). Paul was very intentional in his requests. He did not pray in generalities—"God bless them"—but with great specificity. The more specific our prayers are, the more specific are God's answers to our prayers. Think specifically about what you want God to do for those for whom you are interceding as you pray for them.

Paul wanted his readers (and us) to know "the hope of God's calling." Hopelessness permeated the ancient world, much as it does the modern world. The enemy wants believers to live with an ever-increasing sense of despair. As the Ephesians faced an uncertain future, knowing the hope of God's calling would provide them a sense of security in God's providential care for them. There is nothing in the future of God's children of which God is unaware. The God who saved us is the God who governs the events of our lives. The better we know God, the more we can recognize the counterfeit gods Satan attempts to get us to worship, and the more we can rest in the one true God's providential care.

Pray to Know God's Love and Power

Next, Paul wanted the Ephesians to *know* how deeply God loves them. Satan convinced Adam and Eve they had reason to doubt God's love and concern for them, and the consequences were catastrophic. Satan is the great deceiver, and he does not want God's children to know the depth of God's love for them. He wants them to think, *How can I believe God loves me when my life is so hard?*

You are God's inheritance. We look at ourselves in the mirror and wonder how God could love us (we can be self-loathing), or we wonder how anyone could not love us (we can also be self-loving).[8] We measure our worth by our accomplishments, and they are not very impressive. Yet we cannot fathom what it must mean for God to see a people redeemed by the blood of his Son, indwelt by his Spirit, being conformed into Christ's image, and to know they are his children. When we become more aware of God's deep affection for us, we will stop measuring our self-worth by worldly standards and rest instead in God's love.

---

[8] Both of these are actually forms of pride. Self-loathing is pride deflated (seeking pity); self-loving is pride inflated (seeking praise). But the way forward is not to think more of yourself or less of yourself, but of your self less. Timothy Keller put it that way in "Blessed Self-Forgetfulness" (Redeemer Presbyterian Church: New York, February 24, 2002); which was later published as *The Freedom of Self-Forgetfulness: The Path to True Christian Joy* (Farington, UK: 10Publishing, 2014).

For the Ephesians living in a city saturated with a worldview of unseen spiritual beings, they must have felt great comfort knowing "the immeasurable greatness of his [God's] power toward us who believe, according to the mighty working of his strength" (1:19). Paul stacks up words associated with power to increase the Ephesians' trust in God's power. Their understanding of God's power made available to them would have given them a sense of stability and confidence in their battles against their spiritual enemies—the world, the flesh, and the devil. God's power is actualized in believers through faith (more on God's empowerment of the believer will be examined in a later chapter).

At this point, Paul expands on the concept of God's power given to believers for living the Christian life. This power is comparable to the power that raised Jesus from the dead and seated him at God's right hand. The Christ the church worships is seated "far above every ruler and authority, power and dominion, and every title given, not only in this age but also in the one to come. And he subjected everything under his feet and appointed him as head over everything for the church" (vv. 21–22). God has provided everything we need to live godly lives in this fallen world. The knowledge of Christ's supremacy over the spiritual powers that enslaved the Ephesians before they met Christ would have given them confidence to live for Jesus in a city opposed to the gospel.

When we pause and compare our typical prayers to Paul's prayer, we recognize how much more substantial are his prayers than our prayers (yet I do not mean eloquent or lengthy; see Matt 6:5–8). This thought is not intended to minimize our prayers but to challenge us to pray bolder prayers that are more spiritually impactful. Our prayers need to include matters that go far beyond getting bigger homes and fancier cars, finishing this semester, or seeking help in common illness. These prayers are not wrong, but we need to pray prayers that change others' understanding of who God is so they can live in victory over the world, the flesh, and the devil.

Pray to Be Strengthened by the Spirit

Paul's second prayer for the Ephesians is in 3:14–21. The passage reads:

> For this reason I kneel before the Father from whom every family in heaven and on earth is named. I pray that he may grant you, according to the riches of his glory, to be strengthened with power in your inner being through his Spirit, and that Christ may dwell in your hearts through faith. I pray that you, being rooted and firmly established in love, may be able to comprehend with all the saints what is the length and width, height and depth of God's love, and to know Christ's love that surpasses knowledge, so that you may be filled with all the fullness of God.
>
> Now to him who is able to do above and beyond all that we ask or think according to the power that works in us—to him be glory in the church and in Christ Jesus to all generations, forever and ever. Amen.

Paul knew the Ephesians were in a spiritual war. They needed supernatural strength to battle spiritual foes. Paul demonstrates great humility in God's presence as he kneels before the Father (v. 14). He begins his prayer by praising God as the one "from whom every family in heaven and on earth is named" (v. 15). Paul's words describe God as the source of all life (Acts 17:25) in heaven and on earth. God is the creator of all people, and the same is true of the angelic realm. The fact that a portion of the angelic realm rebelled against God does not change the fact that God created them and reigns supremely over them. An understanding of God's supremacy over Satan and his demons would have been a great encouragement to the Ephesians—the God who saved them rules over their supernatural foes.

The role of the Holy Spirit is emphasized in the empowerment of God's people. We need divine strength as we battle the world, the flesh, and the devil; God provides the source of that strength by giving us the Holy Spirit. This spiritual empowerment should not be understood as some impersonal force, but the result of the believer's union with Christ and the Holy Spirit's work within them. God's empowerment is not according to the Ephesians' needs, but according to the "riches of God's glory." The believer's strength given by God is far beyond merely enough spiritual strength to survive but instead is superabundant (cf. Phil 4:19). If believers are to resist the world, the flesh, and the devil, they need divine strength, and that is precisely what God provides.

When Paul prays, "that Christ may dwell in your hearts through faith," he is not suggesting the Ephesians are not Christians; rather, Paul wants Christ to rule and reign over every aspect of their lives and for them to know in increasing measures the presence of Jesus.[9] The "dwelling" Paul has in mind is not Christ's *taking up residence* but his *residing.* The power of the

---

[9] See Lincoln, *Ephesians*, 206–7; Hoehner, *Ephesians*, 480–82.

Spirit and the ever-growing reality of Christ's presence keep the enemy from gaining an advantage (cf. Eph 4:27).

Pray to Know the Love of Christ

Paul's further request was that the Ephesians would comprehend the incomprehensible—God's love for them. Paul described the Ephesians as "being rooted and firmly established in love" (v. 17b). While Paul mixed his metaphors—one is agricultural and the other is architectural—his point is clear: the roots of their lives went deep into the soil of love, and their lives were built on the foundation of love. Jesus told his disciples on the night he was betrayed, "By this everyone will know that you are my disciples, if you love one another" (John 13:35). Carson puts the matter pointedly:

> The love of God is not merely to be analyzed, understood, and adopted into holistic categories of integrated theological thought. It is to be received, to be absorbed, to be felt. Meditate long and frequently on Paul's prayer in Ephesians 3:14–21. . . . Paul connects such Christian experience of the love of God with Christian maturity, with being "filled to the measure of all the fullness of God" (3:19), as he puts it. It is far from clear that anyone can be a mature Christian who does not walk in this path.[10]

---

[10] D. A. Carson, *The Difficult Doctrine of the Love of God* (Wheaton, IL: Crossway, 2000), 80–81; see further in Carson, *A Call to Spiritual Reformation*, 181–204.

Paul went on to pray that they will comprehend the truly incomprehensible—how much God loves them. The reality of divine love in all its fullness is the result of divine illumination (v. 18). Paul had prayed for the Ephesians to be strengthened in their inner persons by the power of God, and next he prayed they would grow in their understanding of the love of God. To experience the power and love of God at work in the people of God is a prayer worth praying!

God's power and love actualized in believers' lives fortify them against the enemies' attacks. Think about your children or grandchildren for just a moment. Consider praying for them right now to live by the power of God as they face temptations and obstacles in their lives. Pray that they know in an ever-increasing manner how much God loves them.

Paul culminated this prayer with the request that they be filled with all the fullness of God (v. 19b). To be filled with the fullness of God is comparable to what Paul means when he tells the Ephesians to "be filled with the Spirit" (5:18 NIV). To know the greatness of God's power, to comprehend the vastness of God's love, and now to be filled with God's fullness are bold requests.

In case we think these requests are too great, Paul added a doxology indicating God's ability and willingness to do far more than anything we can ask or imagine (vv. 20–21). Considering this reality, one wonders why God's people often pray such *small* prayers. Those living in Ephesus had lived much of their lives in fear of supernatural foes. They needed to understand God's power was available to them for living out their Christian lives. They needed to grasp in a greater way the immeasurable depth of God's love for them. Rather than cowering in fear, the Ephesians could live triumphantly to God's glory by God's power which was readily available to them.

Prayer behind the Scenes

Normally, we are unable to see what God is doing in the lives of those for whom we are interceding. Daniel 10 is a fascinating passage that shows how God is at work when his people pray.[11] We are taken behind the scenes of history and permitted to peek into the relationship of prayer and the unseen world of spiritual reality. The passage describes Daniel's dramatic encounter with an angel. The angel informs Daniel concerning the delay of the answer to his prayer. The passage is straightforward and easy to follow, even though some of the details are perplexing.

Daniel prayed and fasted for three weeks seeking to discern what God was doing on the international scene (vv. 2–3, 14). After three weeks, Daniel encounters an angel (vv. 3–6). Daniel falls into a trancelike state because of the encounter (vv. 7–9). The angel has come to deliver a message to him concerning his prayer (vv. 10–12). Although Daniel's prayer was heard the first day he prayed, the angel's arrival was delayed because of a heavenly battle (v. 13).

The Prince of the Persian kingdom blocked the angel's way to Daniel. We should understand the "prince" to be a hostile angelic power. The term "prince" in Daniel refers to both human rulers (9:6, 8; 11:5) and angelic powers (10:13, 21; 12:1). The fact that Michael opposed the prince strongly suggests, though, "that the prince of Persia" is a demonic spirit. Michael, "one of the

---

[11] This section is based on the corresponding treatment in Cook and Lawless, *Spiritual Warfare in the Storyline of Scripture*, 34–36.

chief princes," intervened, and his intervention allowed the angel to complete his mission. We are not told why the prince of Persia opposed the angel sent to Daniel, but that he wanted to prevent the delivery of a message announcing the downfall of the Persian Empire seems likely (cf. 11:2–3).

How are we to understand this heavenly battle between angelic beings? First, we must realize everything God wants us to know and understand about this passage is provided in the text. Speculation on what we are not told is unwise at best and dangerous at worst. Second, Daniel was unaware of what was transpiring as he prayed. When God's people pray, more may be going on than we possibly understand.[12] Third, Daniel did not pray against demonic spirits but voiced his prayer to God. As mentioned earlier, it is dangerous for believers to speculate behind the pages of Scripture.

---

[12] While the passage is debated, Matthew 18:10 NIV (cf. Heb 1:14) also seems to suggest that believers are privileged because they are represented by angels "who always see the face of my Father," Jesus said. Morris helpfully comments that while the text doesn't say that every little one has a corresponding angel or that the angel is its "guardian," it does describe the fact that angels minister even to the little ones such that "God in heaven is aware of the situation here on earth of even the lowliest of his people." Leon Morris, *The Gospel according to Matthew*, The Pillar New Testament Commentary (Grand Rapids: Eerdmans, 1992), 465; see also Donald A. Hagner, *Matthew 14–28*, vol. 33b of *Word Biblical Commentary* (Waco: Word, 1995), 526–27. Still, while we note this passage may point toward angelic "intercession" (?), two points must be observed: (1) it does this ambiguously (Matthew included this to make a point about the little ones' worth, not the angels), and (2) the NT is abundantly clear that Jesus—God the Son incarnate—intercedes on behalf of his people (John 17; Rom 8:34; Heb 7:25; 1 John 2:1; see also Isa 53:12). Since Jesus intercedes for his people—and his standing in our eyes and the Father's is greater than any angel's, let us delight most in knowing with confidence that Jesus intercedes for us.

What we learn here is that at times it may seem that God has not heard our prayer, or he does not intend to answer it. There were twenty-one days between Daniel's voicing his prayer to God and Daniel's receiving an answer. While Daniel waited for God's answer, much was transpiring in the heavenly places he did not know.

Our prayers make a big impact. Likewise, we must trust God to answer our prayers in his time and in his way. We are not privy to how or when God will answer our prayers. Our responsibility is to pray. We must trust prayer is a crucial weapon for victory over the enemy.

Prayer for the Lost

An important part of intercession is praying for the lost. In a very real way, this is an assault on enemy territory by seeking the freedom of spiritual captives. Paul made this clear when he prayed for the salvation of his unredeemed Jewish kinsmen: "Brothers and sisters, my heart's desire and prayer to God for the Israelites is that they may be saved" (Rom 10:1 NIV). He likewise admonished Timothy to be a man of prayer. First Timothy 2:1–4 reads, "I urge, then, first of all, that petitions, prayers, intercession and thanksgiving be made *for all people*—for kings and all those in authority, that we may live peaceful and quiet lives in all godliness and holiness. This is good, and pleases God our Savior, who wants all people *to be saved* and to come to a knowledge of the truth" (NIV, emphasis added).

One effective way of praying for the lost is using the words of Scripture.[13] Second Corinthians 4:4 reads, "The god of this

---

[13] For help beginning to pray the Bible in general, see Donald S. Whitney, *Praying the Bible* (Wheaton, IL: Crossway, 2015).

world has blinded the minds of the unbelieving so that they will not see the light of the gospel of the glory of Christ, who is the image of God" (NASB). If you were to turn this verse into a prayer, it may sound something like this, "Father, Satan has blinded Bill's eyes. Please give him eyes to see and ears to hear, and a heart to receive the gospel as you did for me."

Another example based on Mark 4:15 reads, "These are the ones who are beside the road where the word is sown; and when they hear, immediately Satan comes and takes away the word which has been sown in them" (NASB). If you were to turn this verse into a prayer, it may sound like this, "Father, Bill's heart is hard to the gospel and your Word. His sinful choices have made his heart callous and unresponsive. I pray your Spirit would soften his heart and your Word would take root and sprout into faith and repentance."

These focused prayers are like calling in a heavenly air strike centered on a particular sinner's heart. In preparation for praying for others, spend a few moments thinking about them to get your heart and mind locked in on them, like a soldier ensuring the coordinates and patterns of his target. As you intercede for people who don't know Jesus, also do not forget the importance of continuing to love them. Remember that they are not the enemy (Eph 6:12); the enemy is the powers who want to keep them in darkness.

Conclusion

When believers do not pray, it is like a group of soldiers choosing not to call in their unstoppable air support in combat. Such believers are usually more independent from than dependent upon Christ. We do not want to be independent from him if we desire to live in victory over the enemy. Therefore, let us not hesitate to call in the divine support of the One who strengthens us to stand firm; let us intercede for others following in the footsteps of Jesus and Paul.

CHAPTER 6

The Presence of the Holy Spirit

As we saw in the previous chapter, the book of Ephesians served as a sort of handbook on spiritual warfare for the church at Ephesus. Numerous passages in that letter emphasize the power of God made operative in believers by the Spirit—God's provision of his presence in our lives. The following passages from Ephesians highlight God's power at work in believers (italics added to each):

- "I pray that the eyes of your heart may be enlightened so that you may know what is the hope of his calling, what is the wealth of his glorious inheritance in the saints, and what is the *immeasurable greatness of his power toward us* who believe, according to *the mighty working of his strength*" (1:18–19).

- "I pray that he may grant you, according to the riches of his glory, to be *strengthened with power in your inner being* through his Spirit" (3:16).
- "Now to him who is able to do above and beyond all that we ask or think according to *the power that works in us*—to him be glory in the church and in Christ Jesus to all generations, forever and ever. Amen" (3:20–21).
- "Finally, be *strengthened* by the Lord and by *his vast strength*" (6:10).

A few observations are in order by way of introduction before we look a little more closely at these verses. First, God's power is not an impersonal force to be channeled but a divinely imparted strengthening of believers to fight spiritual battles. Second, God's power is at work in believers through the working of the Holy Spirit who resides in every Christian. Third, three of these four references to power are situated in the context of Pauline prayers. These prayers were discussed from an intercessory prayer perspective in chapter 5, but in this chapter we will focus specifically on the presence of the Holy Spirit in the believer's life.

Finally, God's abundant provision of spiritual power does not mean that resisting the enemy will be easy or automatic. Indwelling sin, the world, and Satan are formidable foes. Saying "yes" to God and "no" to our spiritual enemies is a battle, but by God's strength it is a battle we can win.

Filled *with* the Spirit

As already mentioned, the indwelling Holy Spirit is how God's power is actualized in his people. One of the most important passages in the Pauline corpus on the Holy Spirit is in Eph 5:15–21. The passage reads:

Be very careful, then, how you live—not as unwise but as wise, making the most of every opportunity, because the days are evil. Therefore do not be foolish, but understand what the Lord's will is. Do not get drunk on wine, which leads to debauchery. Instead, be filled with the Spirit, speaking to one another with psalms, hymns, and songs from the Spirit. Sing and make music from your heart to the Lord, always giving thanks to God the Father for everything, in the name of our Lord Jesus Christ. (NIV)

Paul commanded the Ephesians not to get drunk on wine, but to be filled with the Spirit. Notice how this continues the repeated contrasts of the preceding verses (not/but): (1) not unwise but wise (v. 15), (2) not foolish but understand (v. 17), and (3) not drunk but filled (v. 18). Verse 15 describes the Christian's walk (life) as the opposite of their former Gentile manner of walking (4:17–20), and from this 5:17 concludes that wise Christian living aligns itself with the Lord's will (cf. Rom 12:1–2).

Following these general statements, Paul used a specific example of folly that lacks self-control—drunkenness—to contrast with the wise-walk, which seeks to be filled with the Spirit and so imitate God (5:1–2). As wine is the means by which a person loses his or her faculties and becomes unable to comprehend what is happening, so the Spirit is the means by which a Christian may comprehend and walk in the will of the Lord.

Be Filled

Paul's words should not be understood to mean that believers are not already indwelt by the Holy Spirit. Every believer is indwelt by the Spirit at conversion (John 15:26; 16:7; 1 Cor 12:13; Eph 1:13, 14; 4:30). However, "being filled" with the Spirit and "being indwelt" by the Spirit are two different realities, as Harold Hoehner explains:

> The indwelling, sealing, and baptizing ministries of the Spirit are bestowed on every believer at the time of salvation. There are no injunctions for the believer regarding them because they are an integral part of the gift of salvation. For example, if you are not indwelt by the Holy Spirit, then you are not a believer (Rom 8:9). On the other hand, "be filled by" and "walk by" the Spirit expressed in the present imperative indicates that this is not an automatic bestowment at the time of salvation but an injunction for every believer to follow continually. The filling by the Spirit is more than the Spirit's indwelling— it is his activities realized in and through us.[1]

Paul's command to "be filled with the Spirit" (Eph 5:18 NIV) is in the passive voice, suggesting believers do not fill themselves; only God can fill them. A believer's role is, therefore, better described as "yielding to the Spirit" or "cooperating with the Spirit," as Clinton Arnold writes.[2] The passive voice, however,

---

[1] Hoehner, *Ephesians*, 705 (see chap. 5, n. 2); for further on indwelling and filling, see James M. Hamilton Jr., *God's Indwelling Presence: The Holy Spirit in the Old & New Testaments*, NAC Studies in Bible & Theology (Nashville: B&H Academic, 2006), 127–60, 198–203; Anthony A. Hoekema, *Holy Spirit Baptism* (Grand Rapids: Eerdmans, 1972), 79–93; Gregg R. Allison and Andreas J. Köstenberger, *The Holy Spirit*, Theology for the People of God (Nashville: B&H Academic, 2020), 403–6; Herman Bavinck, *Reformed Dogmatics*, ed. John Bolt, trans. John Vriend, 4 vols. (Grand Rapids: Baker, 2003), 4:87–92; Sinclair B. Ferguson, *The Holy Spirit*, Contours of Christian Theology (Downers Grove, IL: InterVarsity, 1996), 88–89.

[2] Clinton E. Arnold, *Ephesians*, Zondervan Exegetical Commentary on the New Testament (Grand Rapids: Zondervan, 2010), 351.

should not be understood to mean that we merely "claim" the Spirit's fullness or that our moral choices play no role in the process. Since the imperative is present tense, Paul seems to imply the ongoing nature of our need to be filled by the Spirit, in distinction from indwelling.[3] Paul's injunction to be "filled with the Spirit" is similar to his thought in Eph 3:19, to "be filled to the measure of all the fullness of God" (NIV).

What Does the Spirit-Filled Life Look Like?

Scholars debate whether the participles connected to Paul's command to be filled with the Spirit should be interpreted as participles of result (what comes from the filling) or participles of means (ways the filling happens). The participles are translated speaking, singing and making music, giving thanks, and submitting. If they indicate result, then they are *evidence* of the Spirit's fullness in a person's life.[4] If the participles are participles of means, then these describe *ways* believers are filled by the Spirit.[5]

---

[3] Against Frank Thielman, *Ephesians*, Baker Exegetical Commentary on the New Testament (Grand Rapids: Baker, 2010), 358–59, the use of the present does seem significant because it is far more common to use the aorist of this verb in the imperative mood (present: Eph 5:18; [LXX] Jer 28:11, "keep filling the quivers [with arrows]"; aorist: Matt 23:32; Phil 2:2; [LXX] Gen 1:22, 28; 9:1, 7; Pss 71:8; 83:16; Barn 6:12; Pr. Jacob 1:17; TAbraham [A] 4:2; Apocr. Ezek. 5).

[4] O'Brien, *The Letter to the Ephesians*, 394–97 (see chap. 5, n. 4); Benjamin L. Merkle, *Ephesians*, Exegetical Guide to the Greek New Testament (Nashville: B&H Academic, 2016), 175; Daniel B. Wallace, *Greek Grammar Beyond the Basics: An Exegetical Syntax of the New Testament with Scripture, Subject, and Greek Word Indexes* (Grand Rapids: Zondervan, 1996), 639, 644–45; Best, *A Critical and Exegetical Commentary on Ephesians*, 510 (see chap. 5, n. 4.), 510; Hoehner, *Ephesians*, 706 (see chap. 5, n. 2); Lincoln, *Ephesians*, 345 (see chap. 5, n. 4); Thielman, *Ephesians*, 361.

[5] Arnold, *Ephesians*, 351–55.

Just as the phrase "which leads to reckless living" describes the result of being drunk with wine in verse 18, so the participles describe the result of being filled with the Spirit. When the Lord is at work conforming us to Christ by the Spirit, certain fruit is evident (cf. Phil 1:11; Gal 5:22–23). Since the lead exhortation to believers in Eph 4:1–7 is to walk worthy of our calling in unity, and to walk in a Christlike manner is to walk in love (5:1–2), it is no wonder that the fruit Paul gives examples of in 5:19–21 involves praising God together, thanking God together, and submitting to one another out of reverence for Christ.

We should note explicitly, however, that in recognizing these as results Paul in no way means to suggest that believers are wholly passive in being conformed to Christ, like bread that sits for a while grows mold. Since these verses develop and unpack what Paul means when he exhorts us to be careful "how *you* walk . . . *making the most* of the time" (vv. 15–16, italics added), we must understand him accordingly. This seems to be another example of what Piper has called "acting the miracle," meaning that what God must author and do (be filled by the Spirit) we must live out (walk, make the most of).[6] When God authors spiritual resurrection and life in a spiritually dead person who walks in lockstep with the devil (Eph 2:1–6), it is that person who lives and now walks according to God's prepared works (2:7–10). This is the mystery of what it means to actively live by God's strength and not our own (cf. Eph 6:10–18, as discussed in chapter 5).

Returning to the results Paul specifies, two of the participles relate to a Christian's relationship to other believers, and two of the participles relate to one's relationship to God. These are like

---

[6] See John Piper and David Mathis, eds., *Acting the Miracle: God's Work and Ours in the Mystery of Sanctification* (Wheaton, IL: Crossway, 2013).

the first and second great commandments to love God and to love others (Mark 12:29–31). As we pray for God's fullness and choose to live for God's glory, we will experience the fullness of God's Spirit in our lives in increasing measure.

One may interpret Eph 5:19–21 strictly within the context of congregational worship. Thus, being filled with the Spirit is connected directly to participation in the worship of the local church.[7] As God's people gather for congregational worship, the Spirit's work in them becomes evident in increasing measure. If this interpretation of the passage is correct, believers' absence from corporate worship is more damaging to their spiritual lives than they could ever imagine—it would separate them from the people with whom they most naturally grow and recognize growth.

Although the Spirit is actively at work in God's people as they gather for congregational worship, limiting the application of the participles exclusively within congregational worship may be too restrictive. That is, while these are certainly corporate (it is difficult to submit to one another by yourself), they needn't be limited to corporate worship gatherings. For example, rather than interpreting the first participle as related exclusively to congregational worship ("speaking to one another in psalms, hymns, and spiritual songs"), we may see a reference to our speech being filled with graciousness, kindness, and encouragement as we speak to one another.

The "singing and making music with your heart" can likewise be understood to refer to a life that organically praises God—from morning devotions to spontaneous expressions of singing

---

[7] Arnold, *Ephesians*, 361–62.

throughout the day (e.g., driving home from work). For worship to be from the heart is for worship to be genuine and sincere, as believers should be the most grateful of people for all God has done and is doing for them. James teaches that every good gift comes from God (Jas 1:17).

The enemy, on the other hand, wants you to be a person who continually sees the glass half-empty. He wants you to believe nothing ever goes your way, and everyone and everything is against you.

To illustrate, grumbling and complaining have become a national pastime even for some believers (in contradiction to Phil 2:14). As we reject the "acceptable" sins of grumbling and complaining, God's Spirit fills our lives more and more. Finally, as we willingly and lovingly submit our preferences to the preferences of others (Phil 2:3), we are filled by God's Spirit with increasing measure.

An Application

This understanding of being filled by the Spirit recognizes our absolute dependence on God to fill us, while at the same time understanding we do not just sit by expecting an esoteric experience devoid of our personal choices. Thus, what begins in congregational worship continues throughout the week. That means the enemy will fight against us throughout the week, too.

The enemy wants you to speak unkindly and deceptively to others. He wants your mind drifting further and further from God throughout the day, so that you do not break forth in spontaneous worship. The enemy wants you to be a complainer and grumbler, so you are blinded to all of God's good gifts. Finally, the enemy wants you to demand your rights, forgetting that Jesus did not use his divinity to his own advantage (Phil 2:5–11). To fight against the enemy, remember the logic of 1 Cor 6:19–20, "You are not your own, for you were bought at a price. So glorify God with your body."

The fact that "you were bought at a price" has two implications: (1) you are not your own, and (2) you must glorify God who redeemed you. Thus, being filled with the Spirit is not an emotional experience, but an empowerment to obedience, love, and ministry for the glory of God.

The passages following Paul's command to be filled with the Spirit (Eph 5:22–6:9) should not be separated from that command. For example, Paul goes on to say that Spirit-filled husbands will love their wives sacrificially (like Christ loves the church, cf. 5:2). Spirit-filled wives will live in godly submission to their husbands. Spirit-filled children will respect and show honor to their parents. Spirit-filled parents will raise their children in the nurture and admonition of the Lord.

The home is the real testing place of the Spirit's fullness in a believer's life. A Spirit-filled husband will not take his wife for granted. The Spirit-filled husband will lay down his life for his wife by serving her, speaking kindly to her, not taking offense at her, and expressing gratefulness to her for her service to the family. A Spirit-filled father will ensure that his family worships on the Lord's Day, and he puts the spiritual development of his children over their academic and sports interests (1 Tim 4:7–8). The primary purpose of the fullness of the Spirit is not to make us feel good, but to make us godly.

Paul also wrote a parallel passage to Eph 5:15–21 in Col 3:16–17 NASB. The passage reads, "Let the word of Christ richly dwell within you, with all wisdom teaching and admonishing one another with psalms, hymns, *and* spiritual songs, singing with thankfulness in your hearts to God. Whatever you do in word or deed, *do* everything in the name of the Lord Jesus, giving thanks through Him to God the Father."

In this passage, Paul accented the Word of God, while in Ephesians he highlighted the Spirit of God. As we have said earlier, the Word and the Spirit work together to conform God's people into the image of God's Son. Paul included the additional thought in the Colossians passage that everything is to be done "in the name of the Lord Jesus" (Col 3:17). Every aspect of life is transformed from the mundane and filled with the possibility of glorifying God. Paul goes on to demonstrate how this principle is worked out in the world of relationships (Col 3:18–25).

Both Colossians and Ephesians are clear that filling by the Spirit is closely connected to worship and the Word. As we have said previously, what takes place in a congregational context extends to the Christian's life throughout the week. Too many people want a religion of convenience. Too many believers feel no deep sense of responsibility to be vitally connected to their local church. Too many Christians wonder why their teenagers have less and less interest in God, not recognizing they have already been taught that their sporting events and academic pursuits matter more than a vital relationship with Jesus Christ and his people. When Christ does not reign supreme in his people's lives, the Spirit within them is grieved.

Do Not Grieve the Spirit

Paul warned the Ephesians not "to grieve the Spirit of God" (4:30 NIV). Earlier in the same passage, he warned them not to give "the devil an opportunity" (NIV: "foothold"). These verses fall within a section in which Paul encouraged his readers to cast aside the sins of their old life and replace them with deeds of righteousness. The passage reads:

> Therefore, putting away lying, speak the truth, each one to his neighbor, because we are members of one another. Be angry and do not sin. Don't let the sun go down on your anger, and don't give the devil an opportunity. Let the thief no longer steal. Instead, he is to do honest work with his own hands, so that he has something to share with anyone in need. No foul language should come from your mouth, but only what is good for building up someone in need, so that it gives grace to those who hear. And don't grieve God's Holy Spirit. You were sealed by him for the day of redemption. Let all bitterness, anger and wrath, shouting and slander be removed from you, along with all malice. And be kind and compassionate to one another, forgiving one another, just as God also forgave you in Christ. (Eph 4:25–32)

The term translated "grief" expresses the thought of sorrow and disappointment. We should understand all the sins delineated in this passage to cause the Holy Spirit to grieve in the life of a believer. Paul may allude to Isa 63:10 here, which says of the Exodus generation, "But they rebelled and grieved his Holy Spirit. So he became their enemy and fought against them."[8] To grieve the Spirit in this manner would be to fail to learn from the Exodus generation (see chapter 4 on 1 Cor 10), and instead to follow in their footsteps.

---

[8] See S. M. Baugh, *Ephesians*, Evangelical Exegetical Commentary (Bellingham, WA: Lexham Press, 2016), 397–98; Merkle, *Ephesians*, 151–52; O'Brien, *The Letter to the Ephesians*, 345–49.

When the Spirit is grieved in our lives, we should not expect the Spirit to produce the joy of the Lord or the fruit of the Spirit in us. This does not mean we must live perfectly sinless lives to be filled with God's Spirit, but it does mean we must not consciously rebel in our sin. We must seek to put sin to death like greed, anger, critical speech, and caustic attitudes (mentioned specifically in the above passage). When we live in obedience to God by sharing our goods and possessions instead of stealing, speaking words of encouragement instead of criticizing, and demonstrating attitudes of kindness and caring instead of bitterness and resentment, we are living Spirit-filled lives.

A great deal can be learned about a person by how he or she speaks to others and about others. The Spirit's fullness changes the way a believer speaks, as Paul noted in several places in Ephesians:

- "... but speaking the truth in love" (4:15).
- "No foul language should come from your mouth, but only what is good for building up someone in need, so that it gives grace to those who hear" (4:29).
- "... speaking to one another in psalms, hymns, and spiritual songs" (5:19).

Our words, whether we are "speaking to one another" or "singing and making music to the Lord" reveal a great deal about our heart. What we say in our unguarded moments captures a real sense of our Christian character, or lack thereof. Jesus put it this way, "A good person produces good out of the good stored up in his heart. An evil person produces evil out of the evil stored up in his heart, for his mouth speaks from the overflow of the heart" (Luke 6:45). As we put to death the sins of our lips, and the Spirit fills us in increasing measures, our vocabulary changes and the tone of our speech is transformed to God's glory.

Strengthened with Power

God does not leave us to ourselves to live a life pleasing to him. God empowers us to fight the enemy by the Spirit's presence and power in our lives. We examined Paul's second prayer in Ephesians (3:14–21) more fully in chapter 5, yet it merits comment here as well.

The first request in that prayer is for spiritual power: "I pray that he may grant you, according to the riches of his glory, to be strengthened with power in your inner being through his Spirit" (3:16). The power of God is operative in believers' lives by the work of the Holy Spirit. You cannot have fullness of the Spirit without also being empowered by him. Believers should pray for God to empower them by his Spirit to resist the devil, reject worldliness, and crucify the passions and desires of the flesh (see chapters 1–3).

Paul's final request in Eph 3:16–19 is that his readers be filled with all "the fullness of God" (v. 19). To be filled with the fullness of God is to know and more fully comprehend the presence of God, the love of God, and the power of God in increasing measure. To be filled with the fullness of God is to be filled by the Spirit of God unto the fullness of Christ (1:23; 4:13). For the Ephesians living in a dark city like Ephesus, they needed assurance as young believers that God was with them as they fought spiritual battles against supernatural enemies. Present-day Christians also need to know that God is with them, he indwells them, and his presence can be experienced in growing degrees as they walk in obedience to him.

Paul's prayer here concludes with an amazing doxology: "Now to him who is able to do immeasurably more than all we ask or imagine, according to his power that is at work within us, to him be glory in the church and in Christ Jesus throughout all generations, for ever and ever! Amen" (Eph 3:20–21 NIV). Paul's words express the truth that God can do "immeasurably" more in and through his people than they can ever ask or imagine. The power at work in us is none other than God's power.

The final lines of the doxology are somewhat surprising in that Paul mentions God's glory manifested in and through the church and then in Christ Jesus. One might have thought that the order would be God's glory in Christ Jesus and then the church. While we should not make too much of this order, it is not inconsequential that God glorifies himself in and through his church. In Eph 3:10, the manifold wisdom of God is made known to "rulers and authorities" (demonic spirits) through the church. Paul is clear that so much of God's presence, power, love, glory, and wisdom are closely connected to the church. Believers who desire to experience these blessings will not experience them fully apart from active involvement in a local church.

Power in Ephesians 1

This emphasis on God's power running throughout these passages is also found in Paul's initial prayer for the Ephesians. The request reads, "that you may know . . . what is the immeasurable greatness of his power toward us who believe, according to the mighty working of his strength (1:18–19). At the heart of Paul's first prayer for the Ephesians was that they may know God better and better. A growing knowledge of God is not merely intellectual but is experiential as well.

Paul's focus in v. 19 was once again on God's power made operative in the Ephesians. Paul wanted them (and us) to know the "immeasurable greatness" of God's power toward believers.[9] God's power becomes operative through faith. As a Christian's faith matures and his or her relationship with God deepens, he or she is better able to depend upon God's power. Believers need not live in fear or despair as they seek to live obediently to God in a fallen world.

Lest the Ephesians underestimate the nature of this power which is for them (in the sense of "for their advantage"),[10] Paul elaborated on this power in the next several verses:

> He exercised this power in Christ by raising him from the dead and seating him at his right hand in the heavens—far above every ruler and authority, power and dominion, and every title given, not only in this age but also in the one to come. And he subjected everything under his feet and appointed him as head over everything for the church, which is his body, the fullness of the one who fills all things in every way. (1:20–23)

Here, Paul was reminding us that the power of God is on our side. This is the same power that raised Christ from the dead, seated him at God's right hand, subjected everything to Christ, and gave Christ to the church. Christ's heavenly reign is above every demonic power in this present evil age and in the age to

---

[9] See the discussion of God's power in Hoehner, *Ephesians*, 268–72.

[10] Rightly, Merkle, *Ephesians*, 44.

come.[11] The Christ who fills the church with his presence is above all. The Christ who empowers his people is more powerful than all, including the supernatural forces arrayed against the church.

We must recognize that we do not have the power in ourselves to defeat our spiritual foes, but God's power is on our side and for us. This power is the privilege of all of God's children. The power of God is far greater than the power of our enemy—the world, the flesh, and the devil. We depend on it through the Spirit by prayer. Therefore, we must pray to be empowered by God to fight spiritual battles and live godly lives. James said we do not have because we do not ask (Jas 4:2). Let us not be guilty of living a powerless Christian life because we do not ask from God what he desires to give us.

Conclusion

Let us conclude with some practical suggestions. If we want to live in victory over the enemy, we must pray for a greater awareness of the Spirit's presence in our lives. God once dwelt in the Tabernacle, and then the Temple, but now God dwells in his people—corporately and individually (1 Cor 3:16, 17; 2 Cor 6:16; Eph 2:19–22). Consequently, we must be careful to prioritize congregational worship, for to minimize our congregational worship is to damage our Christian life. Spirit-empowered congregational worship spills over into Spirit-filled living in the home and Spirit-filled victories on the spiritual battlefield.

---

[11] Paul expressed Christ's exaltation using the words "far above" (*hyperanō*) to express the dominance of Christ over his supernatural enemies. On Christ's heavenly session, see also Rom 8:34; Phil 2:9; Col 3:1.

Ask God today to fill you by his Spirit. Sing loudly, boldly, and confidently when you gather with your local church body. Listen to your pastor preach, expecting God to speak to you through his Bible-focused message. Throughout the week, worship the Lord as a family and privately as an individual. Read the Word regularly. Speak and act kindly and graciously to others. Reject gossip and speaking slanderously or harshly to others.

Understand your home and work environments are the places where you live out the Spirit-filled life. Reject inward inclinations toward grumbling and complaining, but give thanks to God for all his blessings. Whether you are experiencing a time of testing or a time of blessing, keep singing to Jesus. Our prayer is that the final part of this book will help you keep your focus on him.

CHAPTER 7

The Armor of God

In this chapter, we turn our attention to "the full armor of God" (Eph 6:10–17) that many believers probably first consider when they think about God's provisions for victory. In more than two decades of our studying spiritual warfare, we have found it difficult to recall a book on the subject that does not at least touch on this topic. That makes sense, too, since Paul so strongly reinforces his teachings in the book of Ephesians with this dramatic picture of an armed warrior.

New Testament scholar Francis Foulkes describes Paul's situation this way: "Day by day the apostle, at this time of his confinement . . . was in all probability chained to a Roman soldier. His mind must often have turned from the thought of the soldier of Rome to the soldier of Jesus Christ, and from the soldier to whom he was bound to the heavenly warrior to whom his life was linked by more real, though invisible, bonds."[1] Some writers may give too much time describing the armor of the Roman soldier, but Foulkes's direction is the path this chapter takes. Bill and I (Chuck) want you to turn from that soldier to the "soldier of Jesus Christ." It is in him that we have victory over the enemy.

It's All about God

It is probably accurate to say that Eph 6:10–20 is the best-known biblical passage on spiritual warfare. We often turn there when we are facing difficult battles, and we're reminded then that we're wrestling against principalities and powers. We turn our attention to the devil and his forces because we are experiencing genuine struggles.

That is not, though, where the Bible or the book of Ephesians begins. Indeed, the Bible is not a book about the devil; it is a book about God—marked from the start with these words, "In the beginning, God" (Gen 1:1) and concluding with the words, "The grace of the Lord Jesus be with everyone. Amen" (Rev 22:21). While the devil is a character in the story, he is hardly the focus of the story; God is.

It makes sense then that Paul begins the book of Ephesians with a decided emphasis on God: "Paul, an apostle of Christ Jesus by God's will: To the faithful saints in Christ Jesus at Ephesus. Grace to you and peace from God our Father and the Lord Jesus Christ. Blessed is the God and Father of our Lord Jesus Christ,

---

[1] Francis Foulkes, *Ephesians: An Introduction and Commentary*, Tyndale New Testament Commentary (Downers Grove, IL: InterVarsity, 1989), 176.

who has blessed us with every spiritual blessing in the heavens in Christ" (Eph 1:1–3). Likewise, Paul concludes his letter with a "bookend" that also turns the reader's attention to God: "Peace to the brothers and sisters, and love with faith, from God the Father and the Lord Jesus Christ. Grace be with all who have undying love for our Lord Jesus Christ" (Eph 6:23–24). At best, the devil is only an "in-between" part of a story about God.

Indeed, the first three chapters of the book of Ephesians focus on what Christ has done for us and, consequently, who we are in him. The grace of the Redeemer and the identity of the believer in him reverberate throughout these chapters. He has "blessed us with every spiritual blessing in the heavens in Christ" (Eph 1:3). He "chose us in him," "predestined us to be adopted as sons through Jesus Christ," redeemed us through his blood, granted us an inheritance, and sealed us with his Spirit (Eph 1:4–14). The one who has saved us reigns "far above every ruler and authority, power and dominion, and every title given, not only in this age but also in the one to come" (1:21)—a clear reminder that in him we have victory in spiritual warfare.

We were, of course, in trouble apart from Christ. We were dead in our sin, following the "ruler of the power of the air" and "by nature children under wrath" (Eph 2:1–3). God, though, drew us to him and "made us alive with Christ" (2:5). We are now seated "with him in the heavens" (2:6); we are, by grace, his "workmanship, created in Christ Jesus for good works" (2:10).

In Christ, we have peace and "confident access" to the Father (Eph 2:17–18; 3:12). He has broken down walls of division and united redeemed Jew and Gentile alike, making them one as his body. He has created his church and given them his message "so that God's multi-faceted wisdom may now be made known through the church to the rulers and authorities in the heavens" (Eph 3:10). Again, we find our victory in Christ because he has already defeated the powers. We live in victory not because of who we are, but because of who he is in us. To him be the glory "to all generations, forever and ever" (Eph 3:21)!

Having laid that foundation, Paul not unexpectedly began the passage about the armor in Ephesians 6 with a focus on God. Before he ever brings up the principalities and powers in this chapter (though he has referred to powers and the devil in Eph 2:2 and 4:27), he reminds his readers about the source of their victory. The strength they have—and that we have—comes from the Lord who undergirds them with his vast might (Eph 6:10). His power, not ours, is the source of our victory. In the words of one writer, "Paul's readers will recall that this is the same power that raised Jesus from the dead (1:20) and brought them to life when they were dead in trespasses and sins (2:1). Its adequacy cannot possibly be in doubt."[2]

Even the armor we wear, in fact, is not our armor; it is God's (Eph 6:11, 13). Likely referring to Isa 59:15–20, where the prophet portrays God taking up the breastplate of righteousness and the helmet of salvation as the only one who could save us, Paul makes it clear that God is the source of victory. At no point in spiritual conflict can we find genuine victory apart from our being in the Lord and leaning on his strength. This need to be strengthened by the Lord is a continual one, as the battle is an ongoing one for us—but God has given us his strength, his might, and his armor. We need nothing else to live in victory.

---

[2] A. Skevington Wood, *Ephesians*, The Expositor's Bible Dictionary (Grand Rapids: Zondervan, 1981), 85.

Yes, the battle is real. Yes, the enemy schemes against us, making evil appear "attractive, desirable, and perfectly legitimate [but] it is a baited and camouflaged trap."[3] Yes, the forces against us are many. It is doubtful that Paul intended his list of rulers, authorities, cosmic powers, and evil, spiritual forces (Eph 6:12) to show a hierarchy of the powers, but there is no doubt Paul wanted us to know the intense ongoing nature of the battle.[4] Nevertheless, we are already on the winning side.

Indeed, the Scriptures remind us recurrently that God is our warrior.[5] He sovereignly ruled over the serpent when he sent him to his belly and announced in Gen 3:15 that someone from the seed of the woman—that is, Jesus (Rom 16:20; Rev 12:7–9)—would crush his head. Moses challenged his people at the Red Sea to release their fear and watch as the Lord fought the Egyptians on their behalf (Exod 14:13–14). God gave Gideon and his seriously reduced army victory over the Midianites (Judges 7). David took on a giant who towered over him because he knew the battle was not his in the first place; God would hand over Goliath to the shepherd boy (1 Sam 17:46–47). The prophet Jahaziel reminded King Jehoshaphat and his armies that their impending battle against three allied armies was God's, not theirs (2 Chron 20:13–17). They need not be afraid or discouraged when the Lord was with them as their warrior. Nor do we

---

[3] Klyne Snodgrass, *Ephesians*, NIV Application Commentary (Grand Rapids: Zondervan, 2009), 339.

[4] Chuck Lawless, "The Focus of the Story," Chuck Lawless website, October 31, 2021, https://chucklawless.com/2021/10/10-13-21-amazing -grace/.

[5] See Cook and Lawless, *Spiritual Warfare in the Storyline of Scripture*, 259–62 (see intro., n. 1).

need to fear the battle when the armor we wear is God's in the first place.

Four thoughts are in order here. First, we must remember that God is the center of the story when we study or teach about spiritual warfare. If you finish this book having focused more on the devil than on God, we were not clear enough in our writing or you were diverted in the wrong direction as you read. We want you to experience victory because you know God better, not because you know more about the devil.

Second, focusing on God as the source of our victory should decrease our fear of spiritual warfare. The biblical portrayal of the battle is not a dualistic war between God and Satan as almost equal powers, with the end still in doubt. Rather, it is a war we fight from a position of victory already because God is the warrior who grants us his armor. Even the armor-of-God passage we will review next is hardly dripping with fear; it echoes with victory that is ours through our wearing the armor and praying for one another. As New Testament scholar Sydney H. T. Page points out, "Victory cannot be won without effort, but it can be won."[6]

Third, we also need to recognize that we often lose battles because we choose to fight first in our own strength, and then turn to God only if we must. With regard to temptation, that approach is exactly the opposite of what Jesus taught us to do. His mandate to us was to pray to the Father, "And do not bring us into temptation, but deliver us from the evil one" (Matt 6:13); that is, we are to pray for God's protection *before* temptation ever occurs. When we choose to fight temptation on our own, our

---

[6] Sydney H. T. Page, *Powers of Evil* (Grand Rapids: Baker, 1995), 187.

prayer too often is, "Lord, please forgive me again." We lose the battle because we forget who our warrior is. As the heading for this section says, it really is all about God.

Fourth, any spiritual victory we experience is due to God's intervention and power, so he alone must get the praise. Just as he drove back the Red Sea, empowered Gideon's reduced army for victory, directed the rock from David's sling to the forehead of Goliath, and turned the three armies on themselves in Jehoshaphat's day, he alone is the cause of our victories. Any time we think we deserve attention for our spiritual victories, we've just taken the enemy's bait.

We Must Put on the Armor

We fight the enemy in God's strength and might. The armor we wear is God's armor. He alone is our warrior—but, Paul also told us that we are to put on the full armor of God (Eph 6:11, 13). This tension between trusting the divine warrior and putting on the armor is apparent even while we recognize that God is the center of the story. William Hendriksen's words are helpful here:

> *Man* must equip himself with a full suit of arms, that is, it is he who must *put it on*. It is also *he, he alone,* who must *use* this entire panoply. Nevertheless, the weapons are called "the full armor *of God.*" It is *God* who has forged them. It is *God* who gives them. Not for one single moment is man able to employ them effectively except by *the power of God.*[7] (italics in original)

---

[7] William W. Hendriksen, *Exposition of Ephesians*, New Testament Commentary (Grand Rapids: Baker, 1967), 270.

How, then, do we understand this tension? Again, the entirety of the book of Ephesians helps us. The first three chapters are about who we are in Christ because of what he has done for us. They announce our identity in Christ as "faithful saints" who are chosen, redeemed, forgiven, and sealed. The latter three chapters are about practically living out our Christianity. We are to "walk worthy of the calling you [we] have received" (Eph 4:1), realizing that we are who we are because of Christ—and because we are in Christ, we must live lives that honor him. All areas of our lives—our personal walk, our family, our church, and our workplace—are to reflect the work of God in us.[8] *How* we live out our position in Christ affects whether we live in victory.

Positionally, we are in Christ. Thus, it is accurate at a fundamental level to conclude, "In the context of the letter [of Ephesians], it seems best to conclude that Christ is the full armor of God for the believer."[9] At the same time, though, we practically live out that position in Christ by obeying everything Jesus commanded us to do (Matt 28:20). Our security is in Christ, and our obedience is the evidence of his presence in us. Both aspects—positional and practical—help us to understand what it means to put on the full armor of God. We win these battles by being in Christ and walking in his ways.

This passage about the armor of God is thus not isolated from the rest of the book of Ephesians; in fact, it is both a

---

[8] Chuck Lawless, *Discipled Warriors* (Grand Rapids: Kregel, 2002), 21–42; Lawless, *Disciple* (Carol Stream, IL: Tyndale, 2022), 39–42.

[9] John Gilhooly, *40 Questions about Angels, Demons, and Spiritual Warfare* (Grand Rapids: Kregel, 2018), 163.

summary of the book's content and a challenge for its readers to take appropriate steps to win spiritual battles. As you observe from the text that follows how we summarized these aspects in our previous volume, pay attention not only to who we are in Christ, but also to how we live out Christ in us.[10] Both elements are essential to having victory over the enemy.

Figure 1. Wearing the Full Armor Positionally and Practically

Armor	Our Position in Christ	Our Practice in Life
Belt of Truth	Jesus is the truth (John 14:6).	We must walk in truth as people of integrity.
Breastplate of Righteousness	Jesus gives us his righteousness (Phil 3:9).	We are to live righteously, ever forsaking sin.
Shoes of the Gospel of Peace	Jesus is the good news, the one who restores our peace with the Father (2 Cor 5:17–21).	We are to proclaim this gospel, knowing that beautiful feet do just that.
Shield of Faith	Jesus is the source and perfecter of our faith (Heb 12:2).	We are to trust the promises of God.

---

[10] Cook and Lawless, *Spiritual Warfare in the Storyline of Scripture*, 226–27.

Helmet of Salvation	Jesus is our salvation (1 John 5:11, 12).	We are to live out our salvation as children of God, allowing it to affect our thinking and our actions.
Sword of the Spirit	Jesus is the Word of God (John 1:1–5).	We are to know the Word, live it, and proclaim it.

Victory Is about Lifestyle

Maybe you have heard preaching something like this (and I—Chuck—might have even preached this way myself): "Paul connects the truth to the belt because the belt holds everything up like truth does," or "He uses the breastplate to speak of righteousness because righteousness covers the heart." That kind of application makes for interesting preaching, but it's not likely Paul intended such a focus on the equipment itself. In fact, the apostle sometimes connected a piece of armor to some lifestyle characteristic different from Ephesians 6; for example, he refers to a "breastplate of righteousness" in Eph 6:14 (ESV), but the armor is a "breastplate of faith and love" in 1 Thess 5:8 (ESV). Such varieties show us that Paul did not intend to focus on the armor itself, but rather on the lifestyle characteristic that marks believers. "Truth," for instance, was more significant to Paul than which piece of the armor represented truth.

Moreover, the book of Ephesians before the armor passage is about living out who we are in Christ as a "new creation" (2 Cor 5:17 ESV). God has chosen and redeemed us, freeing us from the power of the prince of the air (Eph 2:2 ESV) and making us new. As those in Christ, we are still "to put on the new self, the one created according to God's likeness in righteousness and purity of the truth" (Eph 4:24). We choose to "walk worthy of the calling" we have received, no longer walking as non-believers do but instead walking in love as children of light (Eph 4:1, 17; 5:1–2, 8). Continually, we pay attention to how we walk, knowing the days are evil and the battle is real (Eph 5:15).

This language of "walking" is about lifestyle. We could, in fact, insert the word "live" for "walk" in the noted verses, and the meaning would be the same. It is not the armor, that is, the specific pieces of equipment God has given us, that give us victory; it is our lifestyle founded on our position in Christ. So, to illustrate, we wear truth because Christ who is truth lives in us, but we also stand against the "father of lies" by "putting away lying" and choosing to "speak the truth, each one to his neighbor" (Eph 4:25). As pastor John MacArthur put it, "Our spiritual weapons can be summed up in one word: obedience."[11]

I admit that some who study spiritual warfare seeking immediate victory over Satan and temptation are often disappointed with this conclusion. When you have lost battle after battle over many years, it is easy to jump at any opportunity for instantaneous freedom—like praying a prayer against a particular demon or seeking exorcism at the hands of a deliverance minister. It is seldom by any means apart from Christian living, however, that we defeat the devil. We submit to God, resist the devil, and repent from our sin. That is a lifestyle of victory.

---

[11] John MacArthur Jr., *How to Meet the Enemy* (Wheaton, IL: Victor Books, 1992), 69.

Spiritual Battle Is Both Offensive and Defensive

Ask other believers if the armor of God is intended to be offensive and you will likely get different responses. Some argue that the language of "stand" in this armor passage (Eph 6:11, 13, 14) has a defensive sense to it, and the word itself does connote standing firm and holding one's ground. Believers are likewise to "resist" and to "extinguish all the flaming arrows of the evil one" (Eph 6:13, 16)—both images that imply a defensive posture. Peter also called us to resist the adversary who is "prowling around like a roaring lion, looking for anyone he can devour" (1 Pet 5:8–9), and James followed suit with a command to "resist the devil, and he will flee from you" (Jas 4:7). It is difficult indeed to read these passages and not conclude that we are to defend ourselves against the enemy's forces.

Some further argue that only the "sword of the Spirit" is an offensive weapon, and the remaining pieces are for defensive purposes. Authors Robert Dean Jr. and Thomas Ice conclude that believers stand firm on the defensive, but it is God who "exercises the option of the offensive."[12] They also argue that viewing the armor as defensive is a needed corrective to those who have focused too much on taking on the enemy: "The ideas of binding, rebuking, performing exorcisms, or taking dominion over Satan and demonic strongholds are *offensive* ideas. When believers go on the offensive against Satan, they are stepping out of their legitimate bounds by becoming involved in situations the Lord has never intended for them."[13]

---

[12] Robert Dean Jr. and Thomas Ice, *What the Bible Teaches about Spiritual Warfare* (Grand Rapids: Kregel, 2000), 155.

[13] Dean and Ice, 154, italics in original.

That concern notwithstanding, the armor does seem to have an offensive purpose as well. Indeed, it is the armor of God— that is, of a God who pursued Adam and Eve when they sinned (Gen 3:8–9), called out a people through whom a Messiah would come (Gen 12:1–3), came himself as the fulfillment of that plan to die for us "while we were still sinners" (Rom 5:8), and promised he would return himself to gather his children to him (Matt 24:29–31).[14] God initiated the plan of salvation and stepped offensively into the darkness to bring redemption.

He created the church against which the gates of Hades could not prevail (Matt 16:18). Our task is to take the gospel to the ends of the earth, making disciples of all the peoples of the world (Matt 28:18–20). We go to the nations because he who came to us first commanded us to proclaim the gospel to all creation (Mark 16:15; Luke 24:47–48; Acts 1:8). Just as the Father took the initiative to send the Son, the Son now sends us (John 20:21).

Offensively, we step into the battle as we seek to make disciples, baptize them, and teach them to obey Jesus. Christian counselor David Powlison summarizes this truth this way: "Often when people envision spiritual warfare, they think 'I'm under attack,' and that is true. Satan does have his wily ways, and he is out to get us. But we are also God's invading army, and we are on the attack. We are bringing light into a dark world. The children of light, the army of light, the servants of light are on the offensive."[15] In Sam Storms's words, "We as Christians should

---

[14] Cook and Lawless, *Spiritual Warfare in the Storyline of Scripture*, 215.

[15] David Powlison, *Safe and Sound: Standing Firm in Spiritual Battles* (Greensboro, NC: New Growth Press, 2019), 20.

never expect to coast, amble, or skip merrily along to paradise. We wrestle! We struggle! We wage war!"[16]

Even the apostle Paul's request for prayer in Eph 6:18–20 that we will examine later in this chapter reveals his offensive posture. When he could have sought prayers of protection, he instead asked for prayer that he might speak the gospel boldly. From the prison cell, he asked the Ephesians to pray he would keep doing what landed him in prison in the first place! No shackles would keep the "ambassador in chains" (v. 20) from proclaiming the good news to those who needed to hear it. No Roman soldier would put him on the defensive; as a matter of fact, prisoners and guards were only prospects to Paul (Acts 16:25–34).

Our conclusion? Clinton Arnold perhaps best states our position: "The heart of spiritual warfare could best be summarized as resistance and proclamation."[17] We are on the defensive as we resist the devil and extinguish his arrows, but the reason he attacks us is because we are on the offensive against him. Thus, we defend as we march forward.

It Is All Connected to the Word

Several years ago, I (Chuck) wrote a seven-week Bible study called *Putting on the Armor: Equipped and Deployed for Spiritual Warfare*.[18] That study devoted one week to each piece of the armor, so it led participants to consider each piece separately. And I would likely deal with each piece in a distinct sermon if I were

---

[16] Storms, *Understanding Spiritual Warfare*, 295 (see chap. 3, n. 11).

[17] Arnold, *Powers of Darkness*, 154 (see chap. 1, n. 21).

[18] Chuck Lawless, *Putting on the Armor: Equipped and Deployed for Spiritual Warfare* (Nashville: Lifeway, 2007).

preaching a sermon series on the armor of God—so I don't disagree that there are different pieces of the armor we are to put on.

No one piece is insignificant, and we ignore any single piece to our peril. If we choose not to wear any piece, we leave a gaping hole for the enemy to attack. He is shrewd—a schemer who methodically seeks such openings—and he aims at our vulnerable areas. Systematically, he tries to weaken us one fall at a time. With each battle lost, we feel as if we have even less strength to fight him the next time he attacks; consequently, a foothold becomes a stronghold.

At the same time, though, Eph 6:11 and 6:13 clearly indicate we must wear the "full" (or "whole"; ESV) armor of God. This mandate reminds us that this battle we face is serious indeed, and the threat of the enemy is alarming enough that we must be fully equipped for the fight. It is possible the list of armor God gives us in Ephesians 6 is not an exhaustive one, but it nonetheless reflects the completeness of the protection God gives us. Wearing all the armor rather than "taking hold of a few weapons,"[19] we are thus ready for the conflict.

More specifically, it seems that every piece of the armor is directly connected to "the sword of the Spirit—which is the word of God" (Eph 6:17).[20] Though the Greek word translated "word"

---

[19] Arnold, *Ephesians*, 444 (see chap. 6, n. 2).

[20] Chuck Lawless devotion, "The Armor of God," Chuck Lawless website, December 9, 2016, https://chucklawless.com/2016/12/120916 -the-armor-of-god/. See also chapter 1 of this book, where Dr. Cook offers this similar summary: "That Word declares the truth which forms our belt (Eph 6:14a), displays the righteousness which is our breastplate (6:14b), presents the gospel which shods our feet (6:15), bolsters the faith which forms our shield (6:16), offers the salvation which safeguards our souls (6:17), and furnishes us as the most formidable spiritual weapon (6:17).

here often speaks of a spoken word more than a written word, New Testament scholar Clinton Arnold rightly concludes "there is really no compelling reason to be forced to choose between these two options."[21] Knowing the incarnate Word and the written Word, in addition to proclaiming the Word, is essential to winning spiritual battles.

It is in the written Word that we discover who and what truth is. There we learn about God's righteousness granted to us. There we read the good news, the gospel. It is through the Word that we experience growing faith, and it is in the Word that we learn God's plan of salvation for us. The Word shows us that we positionally stand in Christ, thus having all the armor of God on us as his strength in us. And it is that Word that calls us to complete obedience while also teaching others to obey whatever Jesus taught (Matt 28:18–20). We stand against the enemy by wearing the armor of God because the Word commands us to do so.

Truth, righteousness, gospel, faith, and salvation are all grounded in the Word—so much so that to separate the pieces of the armor is to miss the point of their unity. That is not to say there are not times when we need to work more diligently on wearing all the armor (e.g., we may need at times to focus more intently on speaking the gospel of peace to others), but we still cannot separate any of the armor from the Word. Indeed, all the armor is so tied to the Word that it seems impossible to win spiritual battles without consistently, regularly, and obediently reading the scriptures. This point is so important that we will spend an entire chapter on Bible study in the next part of this book.

This Word prayerfully employed enables the Christian to stand firm against the schemes of the devil (6:18, 11)."

[21] Arnold, *Ephesians*, 462.

It's about the Body of Christ

I (Chuck) am a big baseball and football fan—particularly, a fan of the Cincinnati Reds and the Cincinnati Bengals. I grew up just north of Cincinnati in a family wrapped up in both teams, so my undying—and frankly, sometimes agonizing—support of them is in my blood. I love the teams, and I'm still excited to cheer for them even though we have not lived in Cincinnati for more than two decades now. I am on their side.

I must admit, though, that I have not always viewed the local church in that "teamwork" way—but I come to that perspective honestly. Many of us in our culture operate individualistically and independently. We have fewer deep commitments to extended families, to affinity groups, or to local support systems than much of the world has. At the same time, we strive to be successful via our personal accomplishments. Put on top of that cultural tendency my own introverted personality, and I too often fight spiritual battles on my own. That approach has never been God's plan.

From the beginning, when God announced it was not good for Adam to be alone (Gen 2:18), the Creator has made it clear he made us to be in relationship with others. He created us needing one another, and he placed us in the family and the church for mutual discipleship and support. Never did God intend for us to be "lone-ranger Christians" who stand in our own strength and fight using our own weapons.

The book of Ephesians, in fact, is addressed to different groups of believers under the Lord's headship. Jewish and Gentile converts alike are united in the gospel (Eph 2:15–16). The believers are to serve together and strive for spiritual maturity, with each member using his or her gifts for the work of the local body (Eph 4:3–4; 12–13). The church is not only the body of Christ, but also the bride of Christ (Eph 5:22–27) and the household of God (Eph 2:19). Both latter images connote the church as family as God redeems us, makes us his children, and gifts us with brothers and sisters in Christ from every nation, tribe, and tongue.

Ephesians 6:10–20 equally reflects the corporate nature of the church. Here, Powlison's words are clear: "The whole book of Ephesians is about the body of Christ, and Paul is not suddenly switching focus in the section on the armor of God."[22] In fact, though our English translations of the Bible usually do not adequately reveal this truth, the commands throughout Eph 6:10–20 are plural. We put the armor on together, stand together, resist together, keep alert together, and pray together. These instructions certainly apply to each of us individually, but as scholar Klyne Snodgrass states, "we should understand them as Paul's instructions for the church collectively to put on God's armor and stand as one person (cf. Phil. 1:27)."[23]

We are one in Christ, in whose identity we stand and in whose power we wrestle to live in victory. Hence, Satan and his minions seek to divide us and to distort our witness. God creates a family, but Satan seeks to make them enemies. God makes us a team, but the enemy wants us to turn on each other. God makes us one in the diversity of the body, but the enemy offers alluring power that turns unity into jockeying for position. Walking in Christ, though, we can stand together in victory. It truly is about the body, as wrestling against the enemy alone is hardly wise.

---

[22] Powlison, *Safe and Sound*, 19.
[23] Snodgrass, *Ephesians*, 339.

We Must Pray at All Times

Chapter 5 in this book already tackled the topic of prayer and spiritual warfare, and another chapter in the next part will offer practical suggestions for growing as prayer warriors who threaten the enemy. We must not, though, leave this discussion about the armor of God without noting again Paul's call for prayer. Professor Graham Cole puts it this way: "The armor of God is not enough without the God of the armor, and prayer is the link."[24]

Our prior chapter about prayer noted the urgency with which Paul emphasized prayer in spiritual conflict, indicated by his recurrent usage of the word "all" in Eph 6:18. All believers need prayer, for all of us are in the battle. The enemy strikes at every child of God, and none of us can live in victory apart from prayer. The combination of our seeking God on our own and others seeking God on our behalf is a victorious one, indeed.

It is striking to me that Paul called the Ephesian believers to put on the whole armor of God before he requested their prayer support. He was in prison, dealing himself with the reality and intensity of the battle, and he wanted to know that his prayer supporters were walking with God. In no way did he desire the sometimes shallow, perfunctory, routine, "it's prayer meeting time" kind of praying that marks so many churches today. Paul did not simply want his name included on the church's prayer list; he wanted prayer warriors who touched heaven and shook hell. The lostness of non-believers was too deep apart from God's grace, and the work of the Great Commission was too impossible

---

[24] Cole, *Against the Darkness*, 169 (see chap. 1, n. 4).

without God's power for Paul to settle for superficial praying. He needed warriors who fought the battle from their knees.

Specifically, he sought their prayers that he would continue to speak the gospel boldly (as we previously emphasized). Paul understood that nonbelievers follow "the ruler of the power of the air" (Eph 2:2), are blinded by "the god of this age" (2 Cor 4:4), reside in the domain of darkness (Col 1:13), are caught in the devil's trap (2 Tim 2:26), and live under the power of Satan (Acts 26:18). They are in bondage to the enemy, hopeless apart from God's gracious intervention in their lives—and even we who are God's children are helpless to make a difference in their lives apart from his power. Nonbelievers caught in the darkness need prayer (Rom 10:1), and gospel witnesses living in the light do, too. Intercession is simply a Great Commission nonnegotiable.

As I write this chapter, I am thinking about several missionary couples around the world with whom I am privileged to work. The missionaries on my team have moved their families—sometimes with preschool children—to the ends of the earth. They work on four continents among various people groups who speak multiple languages. The people they seek to reach generally worship false gods, praying to idols who cannot speak and cannot hear. Some of my team members are aware of national believers who have paid a heavy price for their Christian commitment.

All these folks—my team members and the nationals they work alongside—are on the front lines of the battle. They are light in the darkness, speaking truth in a sea of lies and false religions. They offer peace in the midst of spiritual battles (and literally in the midst of political war at times). Living righteously among peoples often surprised by the commitment their salvation brings, these believers love, live, and proclaim the Word of God.

I know from their testimony that Satan wars against them. He continually schemes to devour them. I love these teammates, and I am honored to work alongside them. Most important to me, though, is my obligation to intercede for them through prayer. I want God to use them as his witnesses, empowering them to share the gospel regardless of the cost and granting them glimpses of his glory as he redeems people around the world. What I *do not* want is for them to operate in their own strength or to lack the prayers of God's people. As I have written elsewhere, "The world to which they are going is a dangerous place—and they want to know they are 'prayer-covered' as they go. This is not the time to only talk about prayer; it is the time to pray."[25]

The battle is too real to send them apart from prayer. We who intercede for them are also too much Satan's targets for us to not have prayer partners ourselves. At the same time, though, we are all *in Christ*. We have God's armor to wear. We get to speak to a God who delights when we come to him boldly (Heb 4:16). He has already broken the powers, and victory is assured. Again, I turn to Arnold for a concise summary statement to conclude this section:

> God makes available his power and divine resources to believers so they can resist the assaults of these hostile spirits and advance God's kingdom into the world. Believers are called to appropriate these gifts, cultivate

---

[25] Chuck Lawless, "7 Challenges from Outgoing Missionaries," Chuck Lawless website, August 25, 2021, https://chucklawless.com/2021/08/7-challenges-from-outgoing-missionaries/.

their corresponding virtues, and above all, pray in the
Spirit as an expression of their dependence on the Lord
to receive God's enabling power.[26]

Conclusion

I suppose it did not catch me off guard, as I had often heard
others teach Eph 6:10–20 the same way: "Here's the way you do
it. Each morning before you get out of bed, pray on each piece
of the armor. 'God, I put on the belt of truth right now. I put on
the breastplate of righteousness. I put on the shoes of the gospel
of peace. I take up the shield of faith. I put on the helmet of my
salvation. I take up the sword of the Spirit.'" The crowd listened
attentively to the conference speaker and generally nodded in
agreement. The process of putting on the armor of God is so
simple, it seemed.

In some ways, it really is not a complicated process. It is
decidedly more than simply praying on the armor every day, but
we have the provisions we need for the battle. God both gives
us his armor and empowers us to live it out. With the Word of
God and the Spirit of God, we march together with the people
of God who fight the battle alongside us. God truly has provided
all we need to walk in victory over the enemy.

---

[26] Arnold, *Ephesians*, 437.

PART 3

Disciplining Our
Lives for Victory

CHAPTER 8

Living in Victory through Disciplined Living

This book is about victory over the enemy. I (Chuck) first studied spiritual warfare in the late 1980s and early 1990s when the topic was gaining great interest among evangelical believers. Back then, conferences and resources that emphasized victory over demonic forces quickly gained traction. They became popular because they often proposed strategies, prayers, and warfare techniques to overcome the evil one—and many, many believers living in defeat were looking in any direction for victory.

Some were longing for healing of difficult marriages. Others had been losing a long-term battle with controlling sins in their lives. Some were dealing with deep bitterness toward others, and nothing they tried freed them from their anger and hurt. The language of "strongholds" became more common, as did strategies for gaining and living in victory. What these strategies often offered were prescribed, quick-fix, formulaic, sometimes eye-catching solutions to breaking strongholds—and they grew in popularity.

Someone losing the battle of pornography, for example, could buy books that included particular prayers to overcome demons of lust. Someone else dealing with ongoing emotional battles might seek to break generational curses through prayer. Others tried to identify "territorial spirits" and "pray them down" in a display of spiritual power. The goal, it seems, was to keep testing warfare strategies until you experienced victory.

I realize that each of these strategies demands evaluating them biblically, but I do understand why someone living in continual defeat might gravitate in any one of these directions. When you're exhausted from losing battles, you look for anything that might finally help you achieve victory. Nobody wants to remain the devil's victim in spiritual warfare, and even one story of victory quickly captures our attention.

Few writers in those days, though, were writing about the topic of this book: that we live in victory over the enemy not by some dramatic, immediately freeing warfare strategy, but by daily Christian living. That is, victory over the enemy comes through obedience, not by warfare techniques. We win daily battles because Christ lives in us, and we follow him faithfully. Critical to that process is the development of ongoing spiritual disciplines, which our friend Don Whitney defines as "those practices found in Scripture that promote spiritual growth among believers in the gospel of Jesus Christ."[1]

---

[1] Don Whitney, "What Are Spiritual Disciplines?" Desiring God, December 31, 2015, https://www.desiringgod.org/interviews/what-are-spiritual-disciplines.

This chapter is about using spiritual disciplines in the battle against the enemy. For now, though, let me begin by telling you some of my story, in hopes you will appreciate why understanding the role of spiritual disciplines is so important to me.

Learning along the Way

I do not claim to be an athlete, but I do run almost every day. I get up quite early in the morning, and I try to be in the gym before it gets too busy. I miss days only when I'm traveling, and even then I try to find a way to exercise wherever I am. Again, however, I do not think I'm athletic.

What I am is *disciplined.* The word itself sounds almost painful, and to be honest, that is not who I am naturally. I am that way now because I spent many years being *undisciplined.* I was active through high school and college, but that changed over the years. I exercised less and ate more—and as a pastor, I ate whatever a church member offered me. At the same time, I slept far too little. I dealt with ulcers early in my ministry when I was undisciplined not only with my physical health, but also with my spiritual well-being. I just did not take care of myself, and I gained enough weight that I was completely out of shape.

At several points, I made a renewed commitment to take care of myself and lose weight. The problem was that I lived on a roller coaster with my health. My pattern was recurrent: work out for a while, stop working out and regain the weight I had lost, make a new commitment to take better care of myself, and start the roller coaster journey all over again. The ups and downs were so many that I had various sizes of suit coats in my closet by the time I had been a pastor for a few years.

Several years ago, the Lord convicted me about my lack of discipline. My dad was experiencing serious health issues related to a similar lack of discipline. My wife and I watched him deteriorate, and we both decided I did not want to follow in his footsteps. Pam, my wife, wanted me around a while—and I wanted to be healthy for her sake. Moreover, I wanted to be healthy as a witness for Christ. He had given me one body, and I needed to take care of it. Now, I work hard to reach that goal.

I wish I could say that my spiritual life has followed a different pattern—that I immediately began implementing spiritual disciplines as a new believer and have continued faithfully on that path for more than forty-five years. That is not the case, however.

My family was not a Christian family as I was growing up, but I heard the gospel from a seventh-grade classmate who cared enough about me to speak truth to me. God saved me when I was thirteen, and everything about the Christian faith was new and unique to me. My pastor gave me my first Bible. He told me I could actually talk to God. He encouraged me to tell others about Jesus. And he emphasized the importance of being at church regularly; after all, he told me long before I understood much of what he was teaching me, "The Bible says in Hebrews 10 not to forsake the assembling of yourselves together."

I had never heard of "spiritual disciplines" at the time, but I was excited about reading the Bible and talking to God in prayer. I jumped in with both feet. Bible reading was amazing (at least through the books of Genesis and Exodus) as I learned about creation, Abraham, Joseph, Moses, Aaron, and others. I really did not know how to pray, so I just mimicked how I heard others pray in Sunday school and worship services. I suspect I sounded much more spiritual than I really was, simply because I echoed the words and phrases of believers much more mature than I was—but it was fun to read and pray. It felt genuinely relational, even for a young teenager, to spend time with God.

Frankly, that stage of excitement did not last long. I was a teenage guy living in a non-Christian home, and my distractions were many. As I moved through the Old Testament, understanding the Bible became much more difficult. Praying prayers that God did not always answer according to my plan made me less excited about praying. Controlling sins that many teenagers faced seemed to hold me in their grip. My passion as a new convert waned, and so did my spiritual disciplines.

Here was the problem, though. No matter how much I was struggling, I still knew I needed to be doing those things because my church leaders kept telling us we should be spending time with God. They *told* us what to do more than they *taught* us how to do it—a serious problem with many churches—but they told us often enough it was hard to ignore their pleas.[2] So I tried to make myself do disciplines simply because that's what God (and my church) expected me to do. What had been a joy quickly became a duty to "check boxes."

Like the way I took care of my physical body, I rode a roller coaster of spiritual disciplines. Some days were good; others were not. When I did "check the box," it was more with relief than with joy. Sometimes, attending a conference or participating in a training led to a high point in my disciplines, but the trajectory soon leveled off. I cannot count how many times I committed myself to get up an hour earlier for prayer and Bible study, only to end that plan by continually hitting the snooze button the next morning.

---

[2] Chuck Lawless, "10 Areas Where We Tell but Don't Teach," Chuck Lawless website, June 26, 2015, https://chucklawless.com/2015/06/telling-but-not-teaching/.

I just was not committed to spending time with God, partially because I still had much to learn about spiritual disciplines.

To be fully honest, it was not until I became a pastor that I began to spend time regularly with God. It was still sometimes a "duty" when I did it primarily to prepare a sermon or write an article, but I slowly began to learn that God wants a relationship with us more than he wants our rituals. I also met some great pastors and lay leaders whose lives exhibited a deep, genuine walk with God characterized by a love for his Word and a passion for prayer. That is what I wanted and needed.

Over the years and because of his grace, God has moved my heart back from viewing disciplines as a necessary ritual to seeing them as a natural part of a real relationship with him. I have learned that it is through growth in a genuine relationship with God that we stand against the enemy, and a healthy relationship is marked by spiritual disciplines. As we noted in the chapter on the "armor of God," an obedient lifestyle rather than a spiritual warfare strategy is the primary means toward victory in spiritual conflict.

Today, I almost cannot imagine going through a day without spending time with God—not because I *have* to, but because I *want* to. One of my goals in this final part of this book is to give you some practical ways to live a life of spiritual disciplines even while I am still learning with you how to do that.

Why the Disciplines Matter

I have already pointed out that many churches tell believers to do spiritual disciplines, but they do not teach them how. Now I add another thought: churches also tell believers what to do, but without helping them know *why* they should be doing it. I am convinced that more church members will be open to practicing spiritual disciplines if the pastor clearly addresses why they are necessary.

While my focus in this next part will be on spiritual disciplines in general, I will make application to victory in spiritual warfare as it's warranted. Understanding why we do spiritual disciplines and how they prepare us for spiritual battles can go a long way toward obedience that brings victory over the enemy.

Disciplines Promote Godliness

The words of the apostle Paul to Timothy, "train yourself in godliness" (1 Tim 4:7), might be few, but they are thought-provoking. In context, the apostle Paul was challenging Timothy to reject false teaching and proclaim truth. One of the ways Timothy could remain focused on the task at hand was to pursue godliness in his own life. With his heart and mind attentive to the things of God, he would show others how to walk with God.

The term "godliness" assumes both right belief and proper action. It carries a sense of reverence and awe, "the active outworking of one's religious convictions."[3] One who is godly thus gives evidence of life transformation, of God's continually conforming him to the image of Christ (Rom 8:29). His life clearly shows that God has rescued him from the kingdom of darkness and transferred him to the kingdom of his beloved Son (Col 1:13). This movement toward godliness is an ongoing

---

[3] Linda Belleville, *Commentary on 1 Timothy*, Cornerstone Biblical Commentary: 1 Timothy, 2 Timothy, Titus, and Hebrews (Carol Stream, IL: Tyndale, 2009), 86.

characteristic of a Christian's journey, beginning with conversion and continuing until the Lord calls one home; it is the process of "exercising one's godliness with the purpose of being more godly."[4]

God makes us holy through Christ's death (Heb 10:10), but living out that holiness requires effort. Paul, in fact, used a sports image to call Timothy to pursue godliness with intentionality and passion. The word translated as *train yourself* is the Greek word from which we get our word *gymnasium*, and it assumes the sweat of hard work to accomplish a goal. Timothy had been trained in the Word since his youth (2 Tim 1:5; 3:15), but still he had to strive daily to live a godly life. He was to use determined efforts to reject false teachings and instead cling to and live out the Word of God.[5]

How do the spiritual disciplines lead us to godliness? Just as food and exercise contribute to our physical health, a steady diet of the Word of God accompanied by conversation with God keeps our attention on the Lord. The Word, as we will see in a later chapter, directs us to sins we must confess, promises we must claim, and daily guidance we must heed. Prayer (another topic we will look at in a later chapter) strengthens us as we live out the privilege of talking with the Creator. Other disciplines likewise turn our attention from ourselves to God—and locking our eyes on him daily should lead to our living more like him each day.

---

[4] George W. Knight, *The Pastoral Epistles: A Commentary on the Greek Text* (Grand Rapids: Eerdmans; Paternoster Press, 1992), 197.

[5] John R. W. Stott, *Guard the Truth: The Message of 1 Timothy & Titus* (Downers Grove, IL: InterVarsity, 1996), 116.

Disciplines Slow Us Down and Put Us in a Position to Listen to God

Maybe your life is like mine—busy. Perhaps, in fact, it is busier than it should be. I serve with a seminary and a mission board. I do church consulting, and I occasionally have the privilege of leading a church as interim pastor. I lead conferences and preach itinerantly. Meanwhile, I write a weekly blog and daily devotion, and I try to keep writing books like this one. My travel schedule, both internationally and domestically, can get intense at times. I confess that my workload—by my choice, most often— sometimes overwhelms me, and I am still learning how to fight for balance even at this stage of my life.

I am not alone here. Kevin DeYoung, in his book *Crazy Busy*, concluded, "Most everyone I know feels frazzled and overwhelmed most of the time."[6] DeYoung argues as well that our busyness hinders our spiritual walk in at least three ways: it robs our joy as our lives are frantic; it robs our heart as we allow the cares of this world to consume us; it covers up "the rot in our souls" because we seldom consider any underlying greater issues that lead to busyness in the first place.[7] I add to this list the argument that our busyness gets in the way of our having personal and corporate time with the Lord.

Most of us are so busy that we have little time to stop, reflect, and just spend time with God; consequently, we often worry more and trust God less. We desperately need that time, though, if we want to be more like Christ. We cannot let busyness—even the

---

[6] Kevin DeYoung, *Crazy Busy: A (Mercifully) Short Book about a (Really) Big Problem* (Wheaton, IL: Crossway, 2013), 16. See also Lawless, *Disciple*, 49–50 (see chap. 7, n. 8).

[7] DeYoung, 26–30.

busyness of "good things"—consume us at the cost of our walk with God. Just as Christ purposefully set aside time to be with the Father (e.g., Luke 5:15–16), we must do the same. Failure to do so results in believers operating in their own strength, churches offering little evidence of gospel power, and communities unchanged by the presence of a Christian congregation among them.

In our busyness, we have also lost the practice of just quietly listening to God through his Word and his Spirit. We listen in general only in "sound bite" moments, and we pay attention only in "between the commercials" segments. Our time with God becomes a brief "we have to do it" activity—not a life-changing time with our Creator and Redeemer. Even if/when we do spiritual disciplines, it's duty more than delight, obligation more than privilege, drudgery more than satisfaction.[8]

Learning to slow down to practice spiritual disciplines with intentionality, purpose, and depth is one step toward correcting these issues. And, lest we fail to consider the seriousness of this issue, God doesn't have to take dramatic steps to slow down our frantic and misfocused hearts if we first deliberately choose to slow down for the purpose of godliness. God does not have to catch us first to slow us down if we set aside time to be with him.

Disciplines Require Us to Manage Our Time Well

I (Chuck) began teaching a class on discipleship and disciple making many years ago, and I learned quickly that most students

---

[8] Lawless, *Disciple*, 34 (see chap. 7, n. 8).

wanted to live disciplined lives—but many had little idea how to manage their time. It seemed they were continually missing deadlines, trying to catch up, and losing the race. For that reason, I now teach time-management principles at the beginning of that class. Not only do I want them to remove excuses that keep them from their disciplines, but I also want them to live wisely in general with each twenty-four hours that God gives them. I pray they will avoid living feverishly to gain what the world offers, only to learn later that what they gained was only fleeting.

Spiritual disciplines take time. Whitney, for example, argues that practicing the discipline of Bible intake requires finding the time to do it (that is, clearing the space each day to do it) and choosing a time to do it (picking a regular time to read daily).[9] Both demand that we use our time wisely to free the time to be with God and daily prioritize our relationship with God to keep these commitments. Doing either is difficult if our plates are already so full that just the thought of adding something to our life is overwhelming.

I say it again: one reason we deal with the busyness we discussed earlier is that we don't discipline our time well. If that is where you are, maybe one of these time-management principles will help you in your struggle with finding time for spiritual disciplines:[10]

---

[9] Donald S. Whitney, *Spiritual Disciplines for the Christian Life* (Colorado Springs: NavPress, 2014), 29.

[10] Chuck Lawless, "15 Time Management Tips," Chuck Lawless website, January 8, 2021, https://chucklawless.com/2021/01/15-time-management-tips/; Chuck Lawless, *Lord, Teach Us Pastors to Pray!* (Franklin, TN: Church Answers, 2020), 13–17.

1. **Review your next day's calendar each night.** Take a few minutes, pray through each scheduled activity, and make sure you set aside some time to be with the Lord—even if it's only a short time.

2. **Get up earlier.** I am not arguing for a certain amount of time or even that you must use the extra time for Bible reading or prayer. But get up earlier and use that time wisely, and you will find extra time throughout the day to be with God.

3. **Use a "to do" list.** This tip surely seems elementary, but I am surprised how little attention some folks give to stewarding their day well. As you work through your "to do" list, be sure to pray as you start each activity, and then whisper a prayer of thanks when you finish it. That way, you will build prayer into your daily routine.

4. **Do less exciting tasks first.** Many of us put off the things we do not want to do. When we do that, we always have something we dread hanging over our heads. If, however, we do those things first, we have more energy to do them—and we'll always have more exciting things to look forward to next.

5. **Use the telephone for its original purpose—to actually talk to someone.** Much of our communication today is by emails, texts, instant messages, or some other means that doesn't require talking to someone. How much time have we wasted, though, when we've had to follow up with these messages because someone misunderstood our meaning or our intent? Most of the time, a simple phone call rather than an ongoing electronic exchange would have saved time (not to mention, too, that there's

just something special about ministering to each other with our voices rather than our typed words).

6. **Use your "10-minute segments" wisely.** All of us can find 10-minute break times throughout the day. We need not use *every* break for spiritual disciplines, but imagine this scenario: three times during the day, take ten-minute segments to read the Word, pray, or both. At the end of the day, you will have spent thirty minutes with the Lord—longer than you might have spent otherwise.

7. **Take care of yourself physically.** In no way can we separate the physical body God has given us from our spiritual commitments. It is tough sometimes to have the energy and the focus for consistent spiritual disciplines when we are out of shape, when we eat poorly, exercise little, and sleep fitfully. Several years ago, I learned from pastor David Platt the exercise of doing devotions while walking on the treadmill. I spend more time in prayer each day beyond those early morning minutes, but now I look forward to spending time with God each day while getting exercise at the same time. There is nothing unspiritual about using your time wisely as you hang out with God.

Disciplines are about turning to God, focusing on him, listening to him, speaking to him, and then telling others about him. Strengthening our relationship with him is both a motivation for and a result of disciplines. If you want to grow in your walk with the Lord even while your growth makes you want to grow even more, make the time to be with him. Doing spiritual disciplines demands that step.

Disciplines Build Our Relationship with God and with Others

I learned spiritual disciplines as the primary means by which I might develop my personal relationship with God (with emphasis on *my* development). I was to practice them daily simply because I wanted to be with God, and the only interaction I had with others was offering "devotional accountability" to a Sunday school teacher, small group leader, or accountability partner. I failed to understand that disciplines can be both personal (like Bible reading and prayer) and corporate (like worship and fellowship)—and they influence our relationship with God *and* with other believers.[11]

On one hand, practicing disciplines demands our spending time with God through his Word and through prayer in the power of his Spirit. In that time together, we find our relationship with God growing stronger and stronger in several ways. First, we turn our hearts from our circumstances and to the God who is bigger than everything we face. No matter how tall the mountains are that we must climb, God is in charge of shaping those mountains. Regardless what trouble we face, God is still in control. Spiritual disciplines are thus lifelines to the Father. Knowing that God divides seas, collapses walls, slays giants, and empties tombs strengthens our trust in Him. No task is too big for our God.

Second, the disciplines remind us of the grace and mercy of God. It is difficult to read God's Word, speak to him, and focus on

---

[11] Whitney, *Spiritual Disciplines for the Christian Life*, 5–6, uses the terms "personal" and "interpersonal," but the concepts are similar. We do this work of walking with God arm-in-arm with other believers.

him without seeing ourselves as the sinners we are. The disciplines challenge us to cry out to God for forgiveness and cleansing—and they remind us that God does indeed forgive and cleanse (1 John 1:9). Reading the Word, praying, fasting, and other disciplines are acts of obedience to the God who uncovers our sin, but who has also already cast them to the bottom of the sea (Mic 7:19). It is necessary and right for us to do spiritual disciplines.

While writing this book, I have been studying the book of Joshua in the Old Testament. This week, I have read again of times the Hebrews entered the Promised Land without driving out and destroying their enemies when they entered the land (e.g., Josh 16:10). God had told them to remove the people in judgment lest their enemies lure them into idolatry, but the Hebrews did not always do that. They instead offered to God only incomplete obedience—which is complete disobedience.

I realized as I read that Word that sometimes I do the same thing. Perhaps I deal with the "big" issues in my life but grant myself some slack regarding the "little" things that displease God. Maybe I obediently pray for someone to be saved but disobediently choose not to speak gospel truth to that nonbeliever. At times, I struggle with things like pride, worry, anger, and discontentment—all among those wrongs Jerry Bridges says have come to be the "acceptable sins of the saints."[12]

Sometimes *my* obedience is incomplete—and the only hope I have is the same hope the Hebrews had: God keeps his Word to his people, holds them in his care, and offers them forgiveness. I knew those truths before my Bible reading for that week, but simply setting aside time to hear the Word again only

---

[12] Jerry Bridges, *Respectable Sins* (Colorado Springs: NavPress, 2007), 6.

reinforced my gratitude for God and his mercy. That's what the disciplines do.

Moreover, practicing the disciplines helps strengthen our believer-to-believer relationships as well. Both Bill and I have already talked about the power of walking with other believers, but it bears repeating again—especially after the COVID-19 pandemic has resulted in some believers pulling away from local bodies of Christ. I remind us again that God created us with a need for him as our Creator, but also with a need for one another as fellow creatures (Gen 2:18). It truly is not good for us to be alone, for God never intended us to run this race and fight these battles alone. In the words of Thom and Art Rainer, "God knows our wiring. He knows that we need someone to encourage us in our personal development. Human existence was never meant to be played in solitude. It is intentionally relational."[13]

Having others in our lives who model Christian living for us also challenges us to do spiritual disciplines. They pray for our consistency and then hold us accountable to our commitments. Others walk beside us as our Paul (a mentor), our Timothy (a mentee), or our Barnabas (an encourager). Indeed, our Paul challenges us to live in faithfulness, our Timothy reminds us that others are watching our lives, and our Barnabas encourages us when spiritual battles are erupting. And, through the study of God's Word, we realize that many others have faithfully walked this course before us—often in much more difficult circumstances than we face. As we grow in our love for God, we grow as well in our love and gratitude for past and present believers who inspire us.

---

[13] Thom S. Rainer and Art Rainer, *Simple Life* (Nashville: B&H, 2009), 69.

Disciplines Put Us in a Place for God to Work in Us and through Us—Including Using Us to Teach Others and Share the Gospel

Consider these statements from others who have written about spiritual disciplines, paying particular attention to the value of disciplines putting us in a place of availability and usefulness:

- "God has given us the Disciplines of the spiritual life as a means of receiving his grace. The Disciplines allow us to place ourselves before God so that he can transform us."[14]

- "Think of the Spiritual Disciplines as ways by which we can spiritually place ourselves in the path of God's grace and seek Him, much like Zacchaeus placed himself physically in Jesus's path and sought Him."[15]

- "We cannot earn God's grace or make it flow apart from his free gift. But we can position ourselves to go on getting as he keeps on giving. . . . We cannot force Jesus's hand, but we can put ourselves along the paths of grace where we can be expectant of his blessing."[16]

- "When through spiritual disciplines I become able heartily to bless those who curse me, pray without ceasing, to be at peace when not given credit for good deeds I've done, or to master the evil that comes my way, it is because my disciplinary activities have inwardly poised me for more and more interaction with the powers of

---

[14] Richard J. Foster, *Celebration of Discipline*, Special Anniversary ed. (New York: HarperCollins, 2018), 7.

[15] Whitney, *Spiritual Disciplines for the Christian Life*, 13.

[16] David Mathis, *Habits of Grace* (Wheaton, IL: Crossway, 2016), 25, 29.

the living God and his Kingdom. Such is the potential
we tap into when we use the disciplines."[17]

In essence, spiritual disciplines move our hearts toward God
in such a way that we are ready to hear from him, live in his transforming power, and obey him. Simply doing the disciplines is not
the goal, however; knowing God is. In the words of Kenneth
Boa, "The disciplines of the faith are never ends in themselves
but means to the end of knowing, loving, and trusting God. As
we implement them in a consistent way, we cultivate holy habits.
As these habits grow, they guide our behavior and character in
such a way that it becomes more natural for us to live out our
new identities in Christ."[18]

When we truly encounter God in this way, he conforms our
heart to his. That is, we develop a Great Commission burden for
our neighbors and the nations (Matt 28:18–20). We live and lead
from the overflow of our personal walk with God, and we can
hardly help but talk about Jesus. Like the graveyard demoniac
Jesus freed from a legion of demons, we tell the cities the story
of God's amazing transforming power (Mark 5:20).

My two pastoral mentors (one who is now with the Lord)
have modeled this kind of evangelistic passion grounded in spiritual disciplines. Both men so live in the Word of God that the
Scriptures rest on their lips. Prayer is so natural to them that you
just know they are friends of God who delight in the privilege
of talking with him. Both have journaled about God's work in

---

[17] Dallas Willard, *The Spirit of the Disciplines* (New York: HarperCollins, 1988), 157.

[18] Kenneth Boa, "What Are Spiritual Disciplines?" *ZA Blog*, January 25, 2021, https://zondervanacademic.com/blog/spiritual-disciplines.

their lives for the many decades of their ministries. They rejoice in Jesus—and that is evident in their readiness to speak about Jesus to anybody, anywhere. Indeed, seldom have I ever spent time with either man when he did not tell somebody the gospel story. For these brothers, disciplined time with God has always led to intentional evangelism toward others.

Disciplines Strengthen Us in Times of Temptation

This point, of course, is directly tied to the point about godliness earlier in this chapter. When the enemy seeks to draw us across the sin line, we have to make some decisions—sometimes over the course of time, but sometimes in the immediacy of the moment. We must determine if we will listen to the enemy's lies and take the bait he has dangled in front of us. We have to decide whether the lure of the temporary or the power of the eternal matters most to us. Given that our enemies include not only Satan but also the world and our flesh, making the right decision is often a battle.

These forces against us are sometimes subtle, sometimes loud; sometimes "in your face," sometimes lurking behind the door; sometimes incessant, sometimes attacking and retreating. Always they are bent on destruction and death. However they choose to attack us, though, we are faced with a few questions. Are we so in touch with God through his Word and prayer that we recognize the enemies' voices? Do we so delight in God because of our time with him that anything the enemy offers us pales in comparison? Do we know the Word enough to recognize that we will reap whatever we sow (Gal 6:7)? Are our conversations with God natural to us, and do they include the cry for the Father's protection against the evil one (Matt 6:13)? The battle is still intense when spiritual disciplines are part of our DNA (perhaps even more intense), but we can still sing "Victory in Jesus" with abandon!

How, then, does practicing spiritual disciplines help us live in daily victory over the enemy? It is simple, actually: disciplines focus our attention on God and our relationship with him. We see him, not the devil. We hear his loving voice over the luring one of the enemy. We experience the undeniable glee of obedience rather than the agonizing conviction of disobedience. We lock our eyes on God—and the enemy loses his influence when our hearts ache more for the never-ending joy of eternity than for the fleeting pleasure of the temporary.

Conclusion

Bill's illustration in chapter 5 of bank tellers and counterfeit bills recalled a similar example in my life.[19] Many years ago, I toured Washington, DC, including the department where the government was creating paper money. I watched from a distance as employees seemed to be playing with paper bills, handling them, testing their ink, holding them up to the light, apparently evaluating them with intentional focus. These were agents trained to recognize counterfeit bills—trained *not* by handling fake money, but by spending sufficient time with real money that they would recognize the difference when counterfeit money appeared. They would know the counterfeit by first knowing the real money well; they would know the fake because they first knew the genuine.

---

[19] I tell this story also in Cook and Lawless, *Spiritual Warfare in the Storyline of Scripture*, 204–5 (see intro., n. 1).

Victory over the enemy follows the same pattern. It is *not* by knowing the enemy well that we defeat him; it is instead by knowing God so well that we recognize when the enemy shows up. We recognize Satan's lies to us because we know well the one who is truth. The disciplines are one means toward knowing God—and knowing him helps us guard against the enemy's arrows.

CHAPTER 9

Living in Victory through Bible Reading and Scripture Memorization

My wife, Pam, and I (Chuck) were in East Asia among a group of believers who had in their possession only one copy of the Scriptures in their language. There were other copies, of course, but these particular believers had only one among them. We watched as this group passed the Bible from person to person, with each one reading a Scripture text before passing the volume to the next person. Their love for the Word was gripping, and their gratitude for having *any* copy was convicting.

When Pam and I returned, we counted the number of Bibles we had in our home. I do not recall the number, but I know we had many more copies of the Bible than we had human beings in our home to read them. We realized just how much we had taken for granted our access to the Scriptures in our language. Frankly, we had failed to see our access as the gracious gift of God to us. The Bible was God's Word, but we had not adequately appreciated it as such. Nor had we understood at that time just how significant the Word is in our spiritual battles. Both of us read the Word regularly, but we did so as much out of habit as out of desire. We still had much to learn.

We in North America have incredible access to the Scriptures in our language. I have been all over the world where believers have none of the Bible in their language—and they sacrifice greatly to hear the Word taught anytime they have opportunity. We, on the other hand, have open access to the Word that we regrettably read too seldom and know too little. One goal of this chapter, therefore, is to guide believers to strengthen their time in the Word as they face the reality of spiritual conflict.

The Power of the Word

How do you typically respond when you face temptation? Try to ignore it? Run from it? Ask others to pray for you? Give in to it? More specifically, how often do you do what Jesus did when the devil tempted him in the wilderness—that is, how often do you quote the Bible?

God does not tempt us (Jas 1:13), but it was the Holy Spirit who compelled Jesus into the wilderness where the devil would tempt him (Matt 4:1–11). As we wrote in our previous volume about spiritual warfare, "God—not the devil—was the initiator in this battle."[1] Indeed, as Keith Ferdinando has pointed out,

---

[1] Cook and Lawless, *Spiritual Warfare in the Storyline of Scripture*, 45 (see intro., n. 1).

Jesus "took the fight to Satan in the wilderness, and there Satan tested the Son of God in accordance with the purpose of God."[2] Hardly was Jesus on the defensive in this encounter; he followed the Spirit's lead as he marched into the wilderness.

For forty days, though, the enemy continually tempted Jesus. We've looked at this encounter in a previous chapter, but we return there again because of the importance of our knowing the Word. The devil offered Jesus the kingdoms of the world, but the Son instead announced through his responses what kind of Messiah he was: he would not choose his own needs over obedience to his Father, he would not do the miraculous simply to tempt God and gain attention, and he would not bow down to the devil. In all cases, he would reject the enemy's lures and obey the Father. Where the first Adam had listened to the voice of the enemy and sinned against God, Jesus walked in obedience to the Father. Where Israel had failed God by grumbling about their food, testing God, and worshiping false gods, Jesus unflinchingly set his sights on obeying God.

For Jesus, the tempter was real, and the temptations were intense. And, in response to all three temptations, Jesus quoted the Word of God. Actually, he quoted the book of Deuteronomy—a book that some of us will struggle locating in the Bible, and even fewer of us will have memorized much of. As a reminder, here are Jesus's responses as Matthew records the story (Matt 4:1–11):

- Temptation #1: turn the stones into bread.
  Jesus's response: "It is written: Man must not live on bread alone but on every Word that comes from the mouth of God" (quoting Deut 8:3).

---

[2] Keith Ferdinando, *The Message of Spiritual Warfare* (London: InterVarsity, 2016), 75.

- Temptation #2: jump from the temple and let the angels rescue you.

  Jesus's response: "It is also written: Do not test the Lord your God" (quoting Deut 6:16).

- Temptation #3: bow down and worship Satan; then gain the kingdoms of the world.

  Jesus's response: "Go away, Satan! For it is written: Worship the Lord your God, and serve only him" (quoting Deut 6:13).

The devil tried to entice Jesus to sin at least three times, and each time Jesus responded with the Scriptures. He apparently did not have a long conversation with the devil; instead, he just quoted the Word. That Word was so deeply ingrained in his mind and heart that he could quickly recall it and stand on its teachings. The Son of God spoke the Word of God, and the devil left him until other opportunities to tempt him arose (Luke 4:13). The battle was not over by any means, but Jesus rejected the tempter's arrows by his standing on the Word.

As we saw in the chapter on the armor of God, the Word of God is an imperative piece of the armor we wear. That Word is life-giving, as Moses reminded the Israelites in his day: "They are not meaningless words to you but they are your life" (Deut 32:47). The Scriptures instruct us in the way of salvation (2 Tim 3:15). They teach us (showing us what to believe and how we should live), reprove us (pointing out our wrong), correct us (putting us back on the right path), and train us in righteousness (showing us how to walk in Christ)—thus equipping us to do every good work God requires of us (2 Tim 3:16–17).

Pastor John MacArthur has written, in fact, that knowing God's Word and applying its principles is the only way to know victory in the Christian life.[3] Donald Whitney makes the same point even more strongly:

> No Spiritual Discipline is more important than the intake of God's Word. Nothing can substitute for it. There simply is no healthy Christian life apart from a diet of the milk and meat of Scripture. . . . Regardless of how busy we become with all things Christian, we must remember that the most transforming practice available to us is the disciplined intake of Scripture. . . . If you want to be changed, if you want to become more like Jesus Christ, discipline yourself to read the Bible.[4]

Thus, the next sections of this chapter will help us read, know, and apply the Word. We will talk about reasons daily Bible reading matters, ways to read and study the Word, and suggestions for memorizing the Word. I will also tell you my method for daily Bible reading, not because it is a perfect method, but because it has been life-giving to me.

Why Bible Study Matters

My journey in reading the Word has been a winding one. When I (Chuck) started reading the Bible as a new Christian, I first did it because my pastor told me I needed to do it. He was my first pastor, and I simply followed his direction. Soon, I found myself fascinated by the stories of the Bible, and I wanted to

---

[3] MacArthur, *How to Meet the Enemy*, 149 (see chap. 7, n. 11).

[4] Whitney, *Spiritual Disciplines for the Christian Life*, 28, 29, 33 (see chap. 8, n. 9).

know more—so I read more. To be honest, though, my time in the Word has often bounced between these two poles: reading the Bible because I am supposed to and reading it because I want to. Maybe your story has been similar.

More recently, I have fallen in love with reading the Word again. As I hope you will see when I describe my reading method, I cannot imagine going through the day without spending time with God in his Word and in prayer. I do not think our spiritual disciplines ought to be "chores" we do so we say we've done them like any good Christian would do, but I do believe we should be reading the Bible every day. Here are some reasons why:[5]

1. **We need nourishment every day.** The Word of God is "sweeter than honey dripping from a honeycomb" (Ps 19:10), and we need its nutrition every day (1 Pet 2:2). Yesterday's reading is not always enough to carry us through another day.

2. **The enemy attacks us every day.** He doesn't say to us, "You know, you haven't read the Bible today, so I'll back off since you don't have the sword of the Spirit ready." He is not that nice—so we need to be wielding the sword (Eph 6:17) every day.

3. **We need to put ourselves under God's teachings every day.** Every day will bring new challenges, new temptations, and new threats to God's Word and his standards. It is far too easy to listen to the clamor of the world

---

[5] Chuck Lawless, "7 Reasons Why Daily Bible Reading Matters," Chuck Lawless website, June 25, 2019, https://chucklawless.com/2019/06/7-reasons-why-daily-bible-reading-matters/.

when we've not put ourselves in a position to hear the Lord's voice that day.

4. **Temptations return every day.** Jesus spoke the Word when the devil tempted him on the mountain, and the devil left him—but only for a while (Luke 4:1–13). Temptation often hits us unexpectedly, and we're seldom thinking about reading the Bible at that moment. We should be daily reading to be ready for any temptation—as it's by knowing and obeying the Word that a young man keeps his way pure (Ps 119:9).

5. **We're different today than we were yesterday.** You might question whether that's the case, but all of us change and grow in different ways each day. That means that a teaching of the Scripture that may not have caught our attention yesterday somehow drives us to our knees today. The Spirit of God knows when we have ears to hear.

6. **Daily reading is an indication of our love and dependence on God.** That's what spiritual disciplines are: a cry for relationship with God and a confession of our dependence on him.[6] When we read the Word, we're saying, "God, I love you enough that I want to hear from you, and I need you so much that I *must* hear from you." Our hearts ought to reverberate with those words every day.

7. **The Word is our way to counter the ongoing, incessant voices of the world.** Let's face it—it's hard to find a quiet place where we don't see and hear the world's ways. It is almost as if temptation stares us in the face

---

[6] I use this phrase to describe spiritual disciplines in general and individual disciplines in particular. See Chuck Lawless, *The Potential and Power of Prayer* (Carol Stream, IL: Tyndale, 2022), 25.

the moment we wake up . . . every day . . . all the time. The best way to counter those voices is to let the Word truly be "a lamp for my feet and a light on my path" (Ps 119:105). Our feet need that guidance every day.

8. **Reading the Word reminds us to keep our focus on God—not on the devil—every day.** From "In the beginning God" (Gen 1:1) to "Amen! Come, Lord Jesus!" (Rev 22:20), the Bible's story is about God and the hero is Jesus. When it's easy to let evil around us overwhelm us and convince us the devil's winning, we need to turn our eyes again on God. The enemy is not winning—and daily Bible reading helps us keep our eyes on God who is the victor.

9. **The Bible directs us daily to the things that really matter.** The older I get, the more I realize how much I've often worried about stuff that amounts to nothing. In fact, I have sometimes stepped into idolatry when I have focused more on the temporary than on the eternal—and I have needed God to redirect me to him. He uses the Word to get me there.

10. **If we truly love God, we will want to hear from him each day.** Just as I long to hear from my wife, Pam, each day, I want to long to hear from God daily. I want everything to feel a bit out of whack and incomplete any day I do not set aside time to be with him. If we truly love him, we will miss him when we do not spend time together.

Practical Suggestions for Reading the Bible More

Some years ago, famous British pastor John Stott wrote, "It is not a casual, superficial acquaintance with Scripture that the modern church needs, but rather to heed our Master's exhortation: 'Let these words sink into your ears' (Luke 9:44, RSV)."[7] Stott went on to say, "There is no particular secret about how to do it. It just takes time, purposefully redeemed from our busy lives, in which to turn Scripture over and over in our minds until it sinks into our hearts and so regulates everything we think and do."[8] That there is no "particular secret" to Bible reading is on target. However we do it, we simply have to do it.

Do you struggle reading the Bible? Maybe you have tried method after method to let the Word sink into your heart, but you have not yet found one that has consistently worked for you. If that is where you are, I want to offer you some simple suggestions to get moving in the right direction. I want you to do *something* in reading the Word, even if you start with only small sections of Scripture.[9]

First, be okay with starting small, and grow in your reading. One reason we wrestle with this spiritual discipline is that we think we must be reading extensively every day or reading not at all; we do not allow ourselves much room for growth in this task. I fear we have been taught that *more reading* is always better than less reading—that is, more chapters are always better than fewer chapters. If reading one chapter a day is more than you have been

---

[7] John R. W. Stott, *Understanding the Bible* (Grand Rapids: Zondervan, 1984), 185.

[8] Stott, 185.

[9] I am indebted to Kevin DeYoung and his work *Just Do Something: A Liberating Approach to Finding God's Will* (Chicago: Moody, 2014) for this concept. I think of it often not only in terms of finding God's will, but of doing any spiritual disciplines. We have to start somewhere.

reading, however, start there. You will never get to two chapters a day until you get to one.

Indeed, quantity of reading is not always best. This formula now reflects my thinking, in fact: "Consistency + quality + accountability > quantity of material." *Consistency* means we read the Word regularly, even if we read only a few verses at a time. *Quality* indicates we read the Word with some intentional depth, and we consider deeply what the biblical text teaches. *Accountability* means we inform others about what we're reading and what the Lord seems to be saying to us through his Word. When these three components of Bible study are present, I do not worry much about *how much* I read at first. What I have learned is that consistent, quality, and accountable Bible reading will ultimately lead to increased quantity in reading.

Second, have a Bible reading plan. I wish I were disciplined enough to get up each morning, determine what I want to read, and let nothing get in the way of my reading. I can quickly get sidetracked, though, while I am determining what to read, so I need to know the night before what I am going to read the next day. *Any* time I spend in determining my reading each new day is an opportunity for something else to draw me away—and for that reason, I want my Bible open to my reading for the day when I wake up in the morning.

Maybe one of these plans will work for you:

- Read straight through the Bible annually (about 3.5 chapters per day).
- Read through the Bible every two years (about 1.75 chapters a day).
- Read one Bible book each month (reading the shorter ones multiple times in the month), thus finishing the Bible in 5.5 years.

- Read through the Old Testament in a year (3 chapters per day).
- Read through the New Testament twice in a year (1.5 chapters each day).
- Read at least one chapter a day and increase your reading as your time allows (but make sure you're using your time wisely, so you have more time!).

While I am convinced that reading through the Scriptures is the best approach, you might also choose to use various short-term methods of Bible study throughout the year. These might include studying a biblical character (e.g., David), doing a doctrinal study (e.g., learning what the Bible teaches about baptism), reviewing famous chapters of the Bible (e.g., the creation account of Genesis 1–3, the "love chapter" of 1 Corinthians 13, or the faith chapter of Hebrews 11), using a devotional book to complement your reading, or meditating on five psalms per day for one month. In my judgment, these methods should be in addition to your reading through the Word—but at a minimum, I want you to begin somewhere.

Third, build accountability into your reading. For many years, I have written daily devotions based on my own daily reading (available at www.chucklawless.com). I began writing them first as emails when I recognized a need to hold myself accountable to my own mentees. I needed them to know what I was reading, and I wanted to encourage them to read with me. It really does matter to me that they know I am reading the Word daily—and I pray that something I write will contribute to their own spiritual growth. No matter how much material you choose to read, communicating with someone about what you have read can help you stay faithful. More on this topic will come later in this chapter.

Fourth, make corporate worship a priority for you and your family, and pray regularly for those who teach and preach the Word in your church. Those who shepherd your church are responsible for leading you to love and live the Word. Their task is a marvelous one—and an awesome one, in the sense of reverence-producing. Lift them up in prayer, and then go to worship with a yearning and expectation to hear the Bible taught. When that happens, you will want to study God's Word more on your own.

Fifth, take advantage of your church's opportunities for studying the Bible together. Given that much of the world has little access to the Word and few opportunities to study with other believers, study the Word with your church in gratitude and humility. Check with your pastor to find out what your church offers. Follow the church's Bible reading plan if it has one. Join a small group that studies the Bible regularly. If you do not want to get involved because you are unfamiliar with the Bible, be honest with the group. Ask for help when the Bible is confusing or hard to understand. All of us have been confused before too. We are all still learning.

Finally, do not give up if you miss a day in your reading. Sometimes life unexpectedly gets in the way of our reading, and we miss a day in the Word. At other times, we wander into disobedience in some area of our life, and we simply stop reading the Bible daily. Whatever the reason for failing to read the Word, do not let the enemy convince you to give up your plan. Simply start reading again the next day and consider getting caught up completely by the next weekend.

A Bible Reading Plan That Works for Me

I (Chuck) could probably write another chapter on the many Bible study methods I have tried and failed over the years. Several years ago, though, I developed a strategy that has reinvigorated my reading. Maybe some or all of it will help you in your own reading.

Each year, I choose a daily reading plan, typically by doing an internet search. I have used different Bible reading methods over the years, but I prefer reading both Old Testament and New Testament materials each day rather than reading straight through the Bible. Though I have used the latter approach several times, I don't like that it is nearly the end of the year before I get to the New Testament.

As I choose a reading plan, it is not imperative to me that I read through the entire Bible in one year. I do, but I do not feel obligated to do so. I do think we ought to read through the Scriptures at least every two years (a little less than two chapters a day), but it is most important to me that we spend some time with God each day. This commitment allows me to focus on the *consistency* element in my Bible reading formula.

Next, I purchase a new study Bible each year. A good study Bible is not inexpensive, but it can help you understand the Word without requiring other resources. I look for a study Bible that gives just enough notes to be helpful—not so many they draw my attention from the Word. Generally, notes that help me understand historical and cultural contexts of the biblical text are most beneficial to me.

Each year, then, I prayerfully choose a set of topics to study throughout the year. This step is the one that has been most important to me, as these topics guide my reading. I always remain open to whatever the Lord teaches me as I read through the Bible, but I especially watch for texts that speak to my selected themes for the year. Among these topics over the years have been prayer, evangelism and missions, leadership, marriage, idolatry, humility, spiritual warfare, gratitude, and many others.

Each day, I enter the Word asking the Lord to teach me something about something.

Simply reading the text, though, is only a start for me. I also
purchase a new set of Bible highlighters for the year and assign
one highlighter color to each of the chosen topics. I note the
colors/topics on the inside cover of my Bible. Always included
among the colors is yellow, which I use for anything else beyond
my chosen topics the Lord helps me to see. For example, the
inside cover of my study Bible for a recent year showed:

- highlights in green: humility
- highlights in pink: peace
- highlights in blue: thanksgiving
- highlights in orange: strength in weakness
- highlights in yellow: other topics or notes that just grab
  my attention during my reading (and sometimes these
  topics become my studies in future years)

As I read each day, I watch for texts related to the chosen
topics. I highlight the text, pause to meditate on it, consider how
it might apply to my life, and perhaps write a few notes in the
margin to help me reinforce the application. With each highlighted text, I pray briefly in response to what God teaches me.
Good Bible study is dialogical, and prayer ought to be our natural response when the Word of God becomes so real to us.

Here, my Bible reading becomes the *quality* reading I want
to accomplish. The Word is convictingly sweet, and it really
does penetrate deeply into the soul (Heb 4:12). It hurts and
soothes at the same time—and I cannot imagine not reading it
every day. To miss my time with the Lord is to miss an opportunity to hear from my Creator and Redeemer. It is to go into

the battle while leaving the sword of the Spirit (Eph 6:17) lying on the floor.

Accountability is the next step. Each day, as I have mentioned previously, I send a brief email to my accountability partners and my wife to show them what the Lord has taught me. That way, they know I have read. They know I am learning. And perhaps they will learn too. Writing the email takes a few additional minutes, but the accountability is huge for me. These emails have evolved into the subscription devotions I now write for my ministry website.[10]

Finally—and this, frankly, is the toughest part of this plan for me—I strive to memorize Scripture out of my quiet time.[11] I still remember the first Bible verses I memorized decades ago. I was a young believer saved out of a non-Christian home, and the Bible was new, fresh, and alive to me then. It still is, and memorizing texts brings life to my quiet time when a verse so captures my heart that I want to remember it. I realize, too, that I may not always have access to my Bible in this chaotic, demonic world; for that reason, I seek to bury the Word in my heart now that I might teach it to others without a physical copy in front of me should that day come.

Moreover, Scripture memorization helps drive the garbage from my mind. I am in my sixties as I write this chapter, but I still occasionally remember ungodly images I saw as a teenager. Out of nowhere come the lures of the enemy as he seeks to draw me into

---

[10] See www.chucklawless.com.

[11] Chuck Lawless, "9 Reasons Scripture Memorization Matters," Chuck Lawless website, July 22, 2020, https://chucklawless.com/2020/07/9 -reasons-scripture-memorization-matters/.

yesterday's sin. The good news is this, though: through the sword of the Spirit (the Word—Eph 6:17), I can capture every thought for Christ (2 Cor 10:5). I want to treasure a word from God more than I revel in the pleasures of the enemy; I want Scripture memorization to help me win today's battles and prepare for tomorrow's attacks so I might not sin against God (Ps 19:11; 119:9–11).

Good Scripture memorization apps are available, but I still use notecards in my pocket to memorize the Word. Wherever I am, I can pull out the card and work on the verse for a few minutes each day. Indeed, the words of Pastor Kent Hughes about Scripture memorization and meditation still challenge me every time I read them: "Even our busy schedules can be punctuated with Scriptural meditation—in the car, at lunch break, or waiting for a bus. Select a choice text, write it on a card, and slip it into your pocket. Pull it out in those spare moments. Murmur it. Memorize it. Pray it. Say it. Share it."[12]

Your goal may be different, but my goal is to memorize two verses each month, using one week during the month to review other texts I have learned. One secret I have learned is that most people—including even nonbelieving friends—are willing to listen as you recite the verse. Children just learning to read will listen, too (and they will often delight when they can correct us a bit!). Not only will others be willing to help you, but they might also learn some of the Word in the process.

This overall approach to Bible study and Scripture memorization works for me, first, because it is a plan; that is, I know each day what I will read. Second, I enter the text excited about what God might show me that day. I do not always find something

---

[12] Kent Hughes, *Disciplines of a Godly Man* (Wheaton, IL: Crossway, 2019), 111.

related directly to the chosen topics, but I always find something that teaches me (which I then highlight in yellow). Third, it really does allow my reading to be conversational as I respond in prayer to whatever the Lord shows me in his Word. I love hearing from the Lord and talking to him in my quiet time.

Fourth, this approach challenges me to keep working on memorization. My pastoral mentors have all been men for whom the Word of God simply proceeds from their heart and lips, and I desire to be like them. I have also learned that memorizing the Word helps us share the gospel. We can, of course, use apps and tracts to evangelize, but having the Word ever on our lips gives us confidence and conviction to tell the good news. Knowing the Word weakens our fears of proclaiming.

Finally, this approach gives me a resource for later use, and— if Pam and I had children—a marked-up, worn-out Bible I could give to the next generations. Even if young people do not appreciate the gift until later in their lives, a used Bible is a good gift to give.

A Word to Parents and Grandparents

For many years now, I have asked students about their quiet time with the Lord.[13] Frankly, many struggle with consistency, especially with Bible study and prayer. Anecdotally, I have learned that the students who struggle least tend to have had parents who modeled quiet times for them. Sometimes they

---

[13] Much of this discussion is found at Chuck Lawless, "4 Reasons Why Your Kids Need to See and Hear You Do Your Devotion," Chuck Lawless website, July 30, 2018, https://chucklawless.com/2018/07/four -reasons-why-your-kids-need-to-see-and-hear-you-do-your-devotion/.

did that intentionally, but at other times it just happened. Their parents did their quiet time in a more public place, and their kids took note.

While I am always hesitant to speak about parenting because I am not a parent, I am certain kids need to see the devotional life of adults they trust beyond Sunday. If all they see happens only on Sunday, they will assume that Sunday is the only day to be with God. Likewise, if the only prayers they ever hear are over dinner or at church, they will learn those are the only times to pray. They need to see that Christianity is a lifestyle, not just a weekend habit—and one of the ways they will learn that Christianity changes lives is by seeing their parents read the Word and hearing them speak to God throughout the week.

Kids also need to hear prayers over them and about them. Even if it seems they are not listening, they need memories of their parents' voices praying for them. As they grow up, they will need to hear those prayerful voices echoing in their heads years later when the world sends them alternative messages. And I am convinced our kids and grandkids really do not grow out of this need. Even in my sixties, I still long for an older adult to put his arm around me and pray for me.

Parents and grandparents, involve your kids and grandkids in your quiet time. You will still need some completely alone time with God, but do not miss the opportunity to invite others to join you. If your preschooler will grant you only fifteen seconds of attention, put him on your lap for fifteen seconds—then tell him a one-sentence story with your Bible open, and say a prayer for him. If your teenager will give you only that same amount of time, pray a Scripture verse over her before she starts the day. Send your adult children an email each day, letting them know what the Lord is showing you from his Word. Occasionally, call them send them a text telling them how you're praying for them.

Build memories into their lives that will encourage them and guide them when they face spiritual battles on their own. Maybe it is a well-worn Bible with Daddy's notes in it. Perhaps it is Momma's prayer notebook that is crinkled over the years. Or maybe it is an electronic journal one of their parents wrote. In any case, it will be a gift they will cling to years later. It will remind them of your faithfulness to God when the enemy tempts them to go in the wrong direction.

Conclusion

My dad became a Christ-follower at age seventy-one after several of us had been praying for him for more than thirty-six years. The Lord dramatically changed him, and he became a model of God's transforming grace for the three years he lived as a believer. Even writing this conclusion makes me miss him and look forward to our reunion in heaven.

Pam and I bought Dad his first Bible—the largest print we could find because he suffered from diabetes that seriously affected his eyesight. The stories of the Scriptures were new to him, and he devoured the Word as much as he could as a young believer. I find it hard to put into words our joy when we saw Dad reading the Word on his own after decades of his rejecting the gospel. He loved the Word, and he loved God more because of what he read in the Word. I have no doubt he alarmed the enemy through his growing excitement and his trusting obedience.

That is our hope for you as you complete this chapter: that you will love God through his Word and stand faithful to him with the sword of the Spirit at your side and in your heart. As we stated in our first book together, Bill and I prayerfully desire that "the Holy Spirit will take God's Word on which this book is based, convict your heart as needed, and draw you closer to him."[14]

---

[14] Cook and Lawless, *Spiritual Warfare in the Storyline of Scripture*, 337.

CHAPTER 10

Living in Victory through Prayer and Fasting

Years ago, I (Chuck) spoke at a conference in a part of the world often marked by strife. The day before the conference ended and I returned home, a local man wounded an American soldier outside a military base. The base went into high alert, and government leaders urged Americans to operate with caution.

Frankly, I was afraid, so I mentioned my fear to one of the local believers. Without hesitation she straightforwardly asked me, "Have you prayed about it?" Her matter-of-fact, simple question challenged me that day more than any of my fears of political trouble did. The Lord used my Christian sister to lay open my heart and call me to repentance.

You see, I *had* prayed about these issues, but not with the childlike, trusting faith my friend exhibited by her question. I prayed because that is what I was supposed to do, not because seeking God was the natural, automatic, first response of my heart. I had preached trust during the conference, but I did not exhibit it when the fire seemed to heat up around us—as evidenced by my rote, weak prayer that day.

I verbalized some words that day, but I did not pray well. I briefly lost the battle with fear. I trust I have learned more about prayer since then (and continue to grow), and I pray this chapter will reflect these ongoing lessons I continue to learn. In addition, this chapter also addresses the discipline of fasting that often accompanies prayer. It is from our knees and in denial of self that we live in victory over the enemy.

The Power and Prominence of Prayer in the Scriptures

Survey the Scriptures and you will see the power and prominence of prayer throughout the text. In fact, we can offer only a sample of the stories here.[1] Beginning with the creation story, we know Adam and Eve had conversations with God (Genesis 3). Genesis 4:26 tells us that the people called on the name of the Lord. Abraham interceded for the righteous in Sodom and Gomorrah, and God intervened to rescue Lot and his family (Gen 18:23–19:29). Moses went before God on behalf of the rebellious Israelites (Exod 32:31–32) and later asked God to show him his glory (Exod 33:18). Joshua prayed for insight when the Hebrews lost the battle at Ai (Josh 7:6–9), and God

---

[1] See similar lists in Charles E. Lawless Jr., *Serving in Your Church Prayer Ministry* (Grand Rapids: Zondervan, 2003), 18; Lawless, *Lord, Teach Us Pastors to Pray!*, 7–8 (see chap. 8, n. 10); Lawless, *The Potential and Power of Prayer*, 13–14 (see chap. 9, n. 6).

directed him to deal with sin in their camp. Gideon prayed for proof of God's leading, and the Lord graciously provided it (Judg 6:37–39). God also gave Hannah a son after she had prayed with great emotion (1 Sam 1:10–13).

Moreover, David asked the Lord's guidance about attacking enemies (e.g., 1 Sam 23:2; 30:8). Solomon prayed for wisdom and later prayed at the dedication of the temple (1 Kgs 3:6–9; 8:14–61). Elijah petitioned God to make himself known before the false prophets of Baal (1 Kgs 18:36–37). Hezekiah prayed for healing and a longer life, and God heard his petition (2 Kgs 20:1–3). Victory came to Jehoshaphat and his armies after the people and the king had fasted and prayed (2 Chron 20:4–28). Both Ezra and Nehemiah confessed in prayer the sins of the people (Ezra 9:5–10:1; Neh 1:4–11); in fact, Nehemiah prayed throughout the book that bears his name (e.g., 1:4, 6, 11; 2:4; 4:9; 11:17). The book of Psalms is likewise filled with prayers, including the psalmist's commitment to pray morning, noon, and night (Ps 55:17).

The prophets, too, prayed. Isaiah agreed to follow God but then also asked how long he must face opposition (Isa 6:1–13). Jeremiah spoke with God about his youthfulness when the Lord called him (Jer 1:6). Ezekiel cried out to the Lord for mercy as God brought judgment on Jerusalem (Ezek 9:8). Like Ezra and Nehemiah, Daniel also confessed sin on behalf of the people (Dan 9:4–19). Jonah rebelled against God's plan, but God's judgment brought him to prayer in the belly of a whale (Jonah 2:1–9).

Prayer was so prominent in the life of Jesus and the early church that I could add another chapter simply listing the examples of prayer in the New Testament.[2] In fact, I am in some ways

---

[2] For other similar lists, see Lawless, *Serving in Your Church Prayer Ministry*, 14–15; Lawless, *The Potential and Power of Prayer*, 47, 50, 57–65;

repeating a list Bill included in an earlier chapter—because it never hurts us to remember how much prayer mattered to our Lord and his Church. Jesus prayed at his baptism, at his transfiguration, and at his death (Luke 3:21–22; 9:28–29; 23:46); thus, he bookended his ministry with prayer. He prayed for his followers and for his enemies (John 17; Luke 23:34). He prayed early in the morning and throughout the day (Mark 1:35; various texts). He prayed alone (Luke 9:18), and he prayed with others (Luke 9:28–29). He rejoiced in prayer (Luke 10:21–22) and grieved in prayer (Luke 22:44). He pushed away from the crowds to pray (Luke 5:15–16), took his disciples apart from the crowds to pray (Luke 9:28–29), and taught them a model prayer (Matt 6:9–13).

The early church picked up on that pattern and built prayer into their DNA. They first gathered in a time of prayer (Acts 1:12–14), and they devoted themselves to prayer (Acts 2:42). When external opposition arose, the believers prayed for boldness (Acts 4:23–31). When internal struggles developed, the apostles and the congregation set apart workers so the leaders could focus on praying and preaching (Acts 6:1–6). Stephen prayed as he died under a barrage of rocks (Acts 7:59–60). Peter and John prayed (Acts 8:14–15). Saul was praying when Ananias approached him (Acts 9:11). Peter prayed (Acts 10:9). The church prayed for Peter's release from prison (Acts 12:5). The church prayed for new missionaries (Acts 13:3), and Paul and Barnabas interceded for new elders (Acts 14:23). Paul and Silas prayed even while they were under arrest in a prison cell (Acts 16:25).

Lawless, *Lord, Teach Us Pastors to Pray!*, 7–9; Chuck Lawless, "15 Ways to Pray like Jesus Prayed," Chuck Lawless website, January 15, 2019, https://chucklawless.com/2019/01/15-ways-to-pray-like-jesus-prayed-repost/.

So prominent was prayer in Paul's life that it is hard to read his letters without seeing his continual commitment to pray—particularly in interceding for others. Phrases like "I always thank my God for you" (1 Cor 1:4), "always praying with joy for all of you in my every prayer" (Phil 1:4), "we haven't stopped praying for you" (Col 1:9), and "I constantly remember you in my prayers night and day" (2 Tim 1:3) echo with the apostle's passion and persistence in prayer. Among other prayers, he prayed for the believers to have wisdom (Eph 1:17), to be strengthened with power (Eph 3:16), to grow in knowledge and discernment (Phil 1:9), and to have spiritual understanding (Col 1:9).

Paul could with integrity call others to "be persistent in prayer" (Rom 12:12), "pray constantly" (1 Thess 5:17), and "devote yourselves to prayer" (Col 4:2) because he modeled a "determination in prayer, with the resolve not to give up."[3] Here is how scholar William Hendriksen summarized this commitment:

> Prayer is the most important expression of the new life. As such it is the means of obtaining for ourselves and for others the satisfaction of needs, both physical and spiritual. It is also a divinely appointed weapon against the sinister attack of the devil and his angels, the vehicle for confession of sin, and the instrument whereby the grateful soul pours out its spontaneous adoration before the throne of God on high. Accordingly, perseverance in prayer is urged.[4]

---

[3] Peter T. O'Brien, *Colossians-Philemon*, Word Biblical Commentary (Nashville: Thomas Nelson, 1982), 237.

[4] William W. Hendriksen, *Exposition of Colossians and Philemon*, New Testament Commentary (Grand Rapids: Baker, 1964), 179.

The Bible not only opens with a relational God communicating with those he created in his own image, but it also closes with a prayer revolving around Christ, the one who is the beginning and the end (Rev 22:13). When Jesus affirmed his commitment to come soon, John responded with a spontaneous prayer of "Amen! Come, Lord Jesus!" (v. 20). The apostle's hope in a dangerous world was the imminent return of Christ, and a simple prayer was his expression of this hope. It was, "as it were, the most that can be prayed. It asks for everything—for all that God purposes for and promises to his whole creation in the end."[5] John thus verbalized in prayer his trust that Christ would indeed come again—and you and I await that return, too. In the meantime, we pray.

The Significance of Prayer in Spiritual Warfare

Why, then, does prayer matter so much in spiritual warfare? First and foremost, genuine prayer turns our attention to God and away from the enemy who attacks us. Particularly when we first begin to study spiritual warfare, it is easy to begin looking for demonic influence and find demons "behind every rock." We can get so fascinated with the devil that we give him more attention than the Bible does—and he at least temporarily wins the battle because we've granted him too much space in our thinking.

Genuine prayer, on the other hand, is, in the words of J. I. Packer, "the active exercise of a personal relationship, a kind of

---

[5] Richard Bauckham, "Prayer in the Book of Revelation," in *Into God's Presence: Prayer in the New Testament*, ed. Richard N. Longenecker (Grand Rapids: Eerdmans, 2002), 270.

friendship, with the living God and his Son Jesus Christ."[6] It is about seeking God, trusting him, and finding our strength in him as we know him more and more. The battles we face are nonetheless real, but it's easier to face the conflict when our eyes are on God rather than on Satan and his forces.

The story of King Jehoshaphat in 2 Chronicles 20 reminds me of that truth. Three armies had allied against the people of God, and the king in his fear turned to God in prayer and fasting. He did the right thing by turning his attention away from the enemies toward the God who could give him victory.

In fact, Jehoshaphat erupted in prayer seeking God's help. In that prayer, he confessed his concerns to God: "We are powerless against this vast number that comes to fight against us. We do not know what to do" (2 Chron 20:12). To feel powerless and clueless when facing a trio of enemies must have been alarming, except for the king's next words in his prayer to God: "but we look to you." Some versions read slightly differently but perhaps more dramatically in describing what the people did: "but our eyes are on you" (ESV). When they did not know what to do in battle, they actually *did* know what to do: look to God as their rescuer.

Locking their eyes on God meant they would no longer lock their eyes on the enemy forces. The king called the people to prayer and fasting, and he modeled those commitments before them. Prayer was both his posture and his power that day; he bowed his heart before God, and God empowered his people to follow the Lord's commands in days of battle. No matter the size

---

[6] J. I. Packer, quoted in D. A. Carson, *Praying with Paul: A Call to Spiritual Reformation* (Grand Rapids: Baker, 2014), 19.

of the enemy's forces, the God to whom the people prayed was greater than all. He still is.

The apostle Paul illustrated this approach in the book of Ephesians as well. As we noted in the chapter on the armor of God, it is not even our armor that we wear in the conflict; it's God's armor. It is in his strength, his might, and his armor that we stand against the principalities and powers (Eph 6:10–12). Thus, we would expect Paul to call the believers around Ephesus to pray as part of his teaching on spiritual warfare; he wanted them to focus on God rather than on the principalities and powers. New Testament scholar Clinton Arnold, in fact, sees prayer as "foundational to deploying all of the other weapons . . . the essence and mode of spiritual warfare."[7] Prayer turns our heart in the direction of victory.

Second, prayer is a confession of dependence on God, that is, a recognition that we cannot win spiritual battles apart from Christ. Again, I am reminded of a story in the Scriptures that illustrates this point.[8] A desperate father brought his demon-possessed boy to Jesus's disciples for healing (Mark 9:14–29)—surely because he had heard that those disciples had cast out demons before (Mark 6:7–13). I can just imagine his growing hope as he made his way to the disciples, but then I can also sense his grief when the disciples failed in their attempted exorcism. Even when Jesus appeared on the scene, the father still struggled with belief after seeing the disciples fail.

---

[7] Arnold, *3 Crucial Questions about Spiritual Warfare*, 43 (see chap. 1, n. 2).

[8] I have also written about this story in Cook and Lawless, *Spiritual Warfare in the Storyline of Scripture*, 243–44 (see intro., n. 1); Lawless, *The Potential and Power of Prayer*, 10–12.

Why did the disciples fail? The Gospel writers tell us that the disciples lacked faith (Matt 17:9–20), and they did not pray (Mark 9:29). I suspect they did not pray because they had already been effective as exorcists in the past, and they assumed they would naturally be effective again. And, when you think you can handle things in your own power, faith in God doesn't matter that much anyway. As I have written elsewhere, they were trying to win today's battles on the basis of yesterday's power; they were operating under the assumption they could do in the present exactly what they had done in the past.[9]

In essence, they were depending on self rather than on God. New Testament professor Sydney H. T. Page describes the scenario this way: "Based on their previous experiences, they probably thought they had divine power at their disposal to use as they saw fit, but in Jesus's view, such thinking evidenced improper faith. Instead of depending completely upon God, the disciples had come to rely upon themselves and their past successes."[10] The result? They could not defeat the enemy who possessed a boy, and they could offer no hope to a desperate father.

On the other hand, prayer says, "God, I need you. I cannot do this on my own, so I am asking you to intervene in response to my prayers." Prayer is, according to Paul Miller in his work *A Praying Life*, "bringing your helplessness to Jesus."[11] That is especially the case when we face spiritual warfare. We cannot defeat the enemy on our own, so we turn to God who has given us his strength, might, and armor to fight.

---

[9] Cook and Lawless, *Spiritual Warfare in the Storyline of Scripture*, 244.

[10] Page, *Powers of Evil*, 163 (see chap. 7, n. 6).

[11] Paul E. Miller, *A Praying Life: Connecting with God in a Distracting World* (Colorado Springs: NavPress, 2017), 43.

Third, intercessory prayer on behalf of others is one of the most effective ways to help each other win spiritual battles. Some years ago, I was teaching a class at a prison. One of the inmates was a strong believer, and he quickly helped me recruit others to learn. During a chapel service when I was speaking about my fear the first time I entered the prison yard, I heard this brother's gruff voice behind me from the choir loft: "We got your back, Doc! We got your back!" His interjection caught me by surprise, but I learned that these believing brothers were ready to take care of me no matter what I might have faced on the yard. They had my back—and I was much more ready then to tackle the task of teaching them. Their support trumped my fear.

That is how I see intercessory prayer partners in spiritual warfare. Remember again that God has not designed us to fight battles alone (Gen 2:18). He has given us brothers and sisters in Christ who stand with us, pray for us, and lift us when we struggle. Indeed, Jesus used plural pronouns in the "Model Prayer" of Matt 6:9–13 that calls us to pray, "And do not bring us into temptation, but deliver us from the evil one" (v. 13). We pray for God's protection for one another, in similar fashion to Abraham's praying for the righteous in Sodom (Gen 18:23–33). Having remembered Abraham's prayer (Gen 19:27–29), God in grace trumped Lot's desire to stay in the city by sending angels to rescue Lot from coming judgment just in time (Gen 19:15–16). Believers who "have your back" really do make a difference in spiritual battles.

Fifteen Practical Ways to Pray

I wish I could say that most believers develop a lifestyle of prayer. It would be great if we pastors could teach believers to pray and everyone would then pray like Jesus, Paul, and the early church did. That seldom happens, however. Even believers who start their Christian journey with a heart for prayer often default into self-dependence in the long run.

Ongoing prayer should be natural for believers, but I am convinced D. A. Carson is right: "The reason we pray so little is that we do not plan to pray. Wise planning will ensure that we devote ourselves to prayer often, even if for brief periods: it is better to pray often with brevity than rarely but at length. But the worst option is simply not to pray—and that will be the controlling pattern unless we plan to pray."[12]

Below are some options for building prayer into your life.[13] The list may seem long, but that is intentional. I want to give you several options, trusting you will choose some to help you pray more.

1. **Establish a focus for each day's prayer.** For example, you might use today to pray for your family, followed by praying for neighbors tomorrow. Don't wonder what you'll pray about each day—plan for it. Calendar it.

2. **Set aside ten minutes to pray, three times a day.** Everyone I know can find ten minutes at different points during the day. We simply fail to think wisely about what we will do with the ten minutes. Choose to pray.

3. **Do "Family Drive-By Praying."** Even on short trips, your family can find prayer opportunities. Pray for other churches you pass. Intercede for school administrators, teachers, and students when you drive by a school

---

[12] Carson, *Praying with Paul*, 2.

[13] I have provided similar lists in Lawless, *Serving in Your Church Prayer Ministry*, 85–96; Lawless, *The Potential and Power of Prayer*, 127–38.

building. Lift up inmates and guards in a prison. Pray for kids on the playground. Invite your children to watch for these places, and they will not miss many opportunities to pray.

4. **Pray as you read the Word.** Think back to my Bible study method I described in the previous chapter and learn to read dialogically. Respond to each text that points out sin or gives a promise. Tell God about things you do not understand. Praise God for who he is.

5. **Pray the ACTS pattern.** If you do not know that pattern, it has these components: **A**doration (praise) about who God is, **C**onfession of your sin, **T**hanksgiving for God's blessings, and **S**upplication (intercession) for others. This pattern gives you a simple starting point for growing in prayer.

6. **Plan spouse and parent/child prayer times.** Christian husbands and wives should pray together every day, even if only for a few minutes. That does not happen, though, unless we plan it. Covenant to pray together at least once every day.[14] Then individually let your children hear you pray for them—and don't stop just because your kids become teens and adults. They, too, need to hear your praying voice.

7. **Spend at least one day a week praying for nonbelievers.** Ask God to open their blinded minds (2 Cor 4:3–4). If you do not know any nonbelievers, pray for people you know but whose spiritual condition you don't know. Pray they will know Jesus. Even in North America, you

---

[14] For a sample spouse covenant, see Lawless, *Serving in Your Church Prayer Ministry*, 89.

might be the *only* person praying for these nonbelievers that day.

8. **Schedule a prayer walk at least once a month.** Find a place in your community where you can walk, look, think, and pray. Pray for people as you walk. In fact, tell your church small group about your plans—let them pray for you as you pray for others.

9. **Pray morning, noon, and night.** You might remember that is what the psalmist said he did (Ps 55:17). Begin the day with prayer, end the day with prayer, and set aside time for prayer at least once during the rest of the day. You might even do what Justin Earley suggests in his book *The Common Rule*: kneel in prayer each of these times during the day.[15] When you pray regularly at these times, you will likely begin to build more prayer into your life.

10. **Listen closely to hear possible prayer concerns throughout the day, and then pray.** Listen to your coworkers, and ask to pray for them when needed. Listen to the news, and then pray for people affected by war and tragedy. Listen to your family, and make sure your prayers for them are more than generic. Listen to God's Spirit, and pray every time he brings prayer to your mind.

11. **Talk to God about everything you do throughout the day.** God's Spirit lives in you. He is with you always. So carry on a conversation with him from the moment you wake up until you lie down at night. It is okay to talk to him about the weather, breakfast, traffic, work,

---

[15] Justin Whitmel Earley, *The Common Rule: Habits of Purpose for an Age of Distraction* (Downers Grove, IL: InterVarsity, 2019), 33–44.

sports, cars, gardens, dreams, goals, supper . . . and on
and on. I *love* an ongoing conversation with God who
loves me.

12. **Pray through your small group or church member-
    ship list.** Everybody in your small group and church,
    including those who are inactive, needs your prayers.
    Schedule to pray through names every day so that you
    pray for each small group or church family at least once
    a quarter.

13. **Send a prayer text or email each day to someone.** As
    you pray throughout the day, send a prayer message to
    at least one person. Writing it will not take long, but the
    benefits of sending it could last a long time.

14. **Pray as you walk through your church facility each
    week.** Whisper a prayer for folks you greet. Pray for
    groups that meet in each room. Intercede for the pastors
    and the congregation as you enter the worship center
    (and, if your church is like many others, you can focus
    your praying since many folks sit in the same seat each
    week!).

15. **Use a prayer globe or prayer map in your home.** Once a
    week, introduce your family to another part of the world.
    Show them the location on the globe. Tell them about
    the people there, including whether they know Jesus.
    Pray for the people and for missionaries who may be
    serving there.

Take time now to decide which of these ideas might prove
most helpful to you. Don't just read through this list; instead,
prayerfully commit to strengthen your prayer life in the days
to come.

The Role of Fasting in a Believer's Life

I (Chuck) was a young believer the first time I heard about a "fellowship dinner."[16] Church was new to me, so I asked others about this event. What I learned is that church members bring more food than anyone can eat, and everyone feasts on the various options . . . like salads, mashed potatoes, sweet corn, green beans, roast beef, fried chicken, meatloaf, bread, rolls, cookies, cakes, meringue pies, and sometimes homemade ice cream. I decided early on in my Christian walk that I really liked fellowship dinners!

Imagine my confusion, then, when I later learned about fasting, a discipline Don Whitney defines as "a Christian's voluntary abstinence from food for spiritual purposes."[17] I liked the idea of eating a lot, but *not* eating made little sense to me. And, at the same time, my church only briefly and occasionally talked about this discipline. I am convinced most of them were not interested in not eating, either. Still, I could not ignore the Scriptures.

Space doesn't allow a lengthy discussion here of biblical examples of fasting, but perhaps these words from author Richard Foster, in addition to the summary that follows in the next paragraphs, will challenge you to fast: "The list of biblical personages who fasted reads like a 'Who's Who' of Scripture: Moses the lawgiver, David the king, Elijah the prophet, Esther the queen, Daniel the seer, Anna the prophetess, Paul the apostle, Jesus Christ the incarnate Son."[18] Foster then rightly adds,

---

[16] See Lawless, *Discipled Warriors*, 169–70 (see chap. 7, n. 8).

[17] Whitney, *Spiritual Disciplines for the Christian Life*, 160 (see chap. 8, n. 9).

[18] Richard J. Foster, *Celebration of Discipline: The Path to Spiritual Growth* (New York: HarperCollins, 2003), 48.

"Fasting reminds us that we are sustained 'by every word that proceeds from the mouth of God' (Matt. 4:4). Food does not sustain us; God sustains us."[19]

In the Old Testament, the followers of God fasted on the Day of Atonement (Lev 16:29–31), when the people sought God's forgiveness through sacrifices. They also fasted in times of national crisis or renewal (e.g., King Jehoshaphat's call for fasting in 2 Chron 20:3, Esther's call for a fast in Esth 4:16, and Nehemiah's challenge to fast in Neh 9:1). Nehemiah also fasted over the condition of the walls of Jerusalem (Neh 1:4). Daniel completed a partial fast while in captivity in Babylon (Dan 1:11–16), and he followed later by fasting over his own sin and the sins of others (Dan 9:3).

The early church likewise fasted when they made major decisions like commissioning the first missionaries (Acts 13:2–3) and choosing the first elders (Acts 14:23). More importantly, Jesus assumed his followers would fast. He did not give them extensive directions, but he did speak of their ongoing fasting in the same discussion about their ongoing giving and praying (Matt 6:2–3, 5–7, 16–17). Just as they continued to give and pray, they were to continue to fast. They were not to make a spectacle of themselves when they fasted, but they were indeed to do it.

At the same time, however, it appears Jesus's disciples were *not* fasting when he was with them (Matt 9:14–17). Even the disciples of John fasted, and they could not figure out why Jesus's disciples did not. Jesus's explanation for their actions, an explanation pastor John Piper has called "the most important word

---

[19] Foster, 55.

on fasting in the Bible"[20] was, "Can the wedding guests be sad while the groom is with them? The time will come when the groom will be taken away from them, and then they will fast." Fasting had no place when Jesus was physically present with his disciples, but they would fast after he had returned to the Father. That fasting would be a heartfelt pining for the Lord; in that day, they would so long for Christ to return that little else mattered—including food.

Fasting is about longing to know God more, as Piper says: "This is the essence of Christian fasting: We ache and yearn—and fast—to know more and more of all that God is for us in Jesus."[21] Fasting says, "God, I love you and long to know you more intimately. I long for you to come again." It pushes away from the table and looks instead to the Redeemer, and your desire to eat then loses its force when you desire God more than anything. As I once heard a seminary president say, "Fasting is about wanting to eat at God's table more than at our own table."

Why, then, should we fast if we want to live in victory over the enemy? We have already noted that the Bible assumes we will fast—and obedience to the teachings of the Word will guard against the enemy's attacks. Think about these additional reasons as well:[22]

---

[20] John Piper, *A Hunger for God: Desiring God through Fasting and Prayer* (Wheaton, IL: Crossway, 1997), 34.

[21] Piper, 48.

[22] Chuck Lawless, "8 Reasons Leaders Should Be Fasting," Chuck Lawless website, October 31, 2019, https://chucklawless.com/2019/10/8-reasons-leaders-should-be-fasting/.

1. **Fasting requires us to focus on God's kingdom.** The kingdom of God is already here (Luke 11:20), but also yet to come (Luke 22:18). We fast while we wait for the bridegroom to return for his bride, and doing so requires us to focus on his kingdom—not ours. Fasting might even show us when we are wrongly building our own kingdom.

2. **Fasting leads us to slow down and reflect.** Doing church usually means activity and busyness. Always there is something else to complete, somebody to visit, the next meeting to conduct or attend, another study to read or teach. Often left behind is our private, personal, intimate walk with God. Fasting is one means to redirect our attention to him as we step away from the table to be with him.

3. **Fasting calls us to consider our deepest longings.** We do not fast to "get stuff" from God; we fast because we want *God himself* more than anything else. Fasting exposes whether we truly believe encountering the eternal one is more significant than the temporary satisfaction of food. It forces us to determine what we really live for.

4. **Fasting reveals who we really are.** It was again Piper who taught me this truth.[23] When hunger consumes us during fasting, we sometimes find ourselves grumpy, short-tempered, anxious, or faithless. To state it a better way, fasting brings to light our true self. Most of the time, repentance becomes the next necessary step.

5. **Fasting should increase our praying.** I love the way Charles Spurgeon united these disciplines: "There is

---

[23] John Piper, "What Is the Purpose of Fasting?" Desiring God, April 18, 2013, https://www.desiringgod.org/interviews/what-is-the-purpose-of-fasting.

a mighty effectiveness in these two gospel ordinances of prayer and fasting. The first links us to heaven; the second separates us from earth. Prayer takes us to the banqueting table of God; fasting overturns the indulgent tables of earth. Prayer allows us to feed on the Bread of Heaven, and fasting delivers our spirits from being encumbered with the fullness of bread that perishes."[24]

6. **Fasting is a reminder we are not as strong as we think we are.** Church leaders are often by nature tough, persistent, and resilient. Fasting, however, quickly reveals our limitations. Denying self for a short fast is not easy, and a longer fast shows our weakness even more. All our knowledge, training, experience, and positions mean little when our body cries out for food.

7. **Fasting is about denying self—the opposite of the enemy's desire that we magnify self.** This discipline focuses on food, but it also pushes us to evaluate where other appetites are out of control as we focus on God. Those appetites become apparent when we replace our eating with other potential idols like social media, television, the internet, sports, dollars, and jobs.

My own commitment is to fast at least one full day per month, and I also typically turn to a fast when something in my life makes me long for God and his intervention. That "something in my life" is typically a need for which I am praying, and fasting reminds me to keep my attention on God who is the source of the answers. For example, I fast for at least a day when

---

[24] Charles Spurgeon, *Spurgeon on Prayer & Spiritual Warfare* (New Kensington, PA: Whitaker House, 1998), 364.

I am deeply, painfully burdened over nonbelieving family and friends. I want God to save them more than I want to eat.

If you have made a commitment to fast more, start small—for example, fasting from only one meal per week. Use that time instead to focus on God through Bible study and prayer. Do not announce your commitment to fast, but do tell someone who will pray for you during your fast. If you fail the fast, prayerfully seek God again in the days to come—do not let the enemy's arrows rob you of the joy of fasting. Start again and seek God more than anything. The enemy will flee when you submit to God (Jas 4:7).

Conclusion

As I finish this chapter, the television is on in the background. I have not been paying much attention to the show, but I have been drawn to several commercials over the last few hours. Advertisers use these commercials to convince us of at least three things: that we deserve something, that we will be missing something if we don't go get it, and that we need to go get it now. Some of the commercials relate to restaurants and food, and their goal is to make us hungry enough to go get the food. At least in the world of marketing, a commercial that leads us to quickly buy something for ourselves is an effective one.

The world's philosophy is simple. Live for yourself. Get what you deserve. Take what you can take. Eat until you're beyond full. Do whatever you want. How different that is from followers of Jesus Christ who live for Christ, rely fully on him, and even deny self to focus on him. Somehow, in the surrender of ourselves through prayer and fasting, we defeat the enemy. Victory comes when God is the focus of all we do.

CHAPTER 11

Helping Others
Live in Victory

This book has been about living in victory—about defeating the world, the flesh, and the devil. This part has focused on victory through strong spiritual disciplines. Bill and I have already discussed in this book the importance of having other believers in our lives, but I still wonder if we have emphasized strongly enough the necessity of fighting the battle *together*. It is easy to emphasize individual and personal victory without thinking much about helping each other defeat the enemy. And, when our focus is primarily on self, the enemy is already winning at some level.

We want to address this issue in this chapter so that you, our readers, will recognize the necessity of walking with others in this conflict. Here's the picture that most comes to mind for me when I think about this responsibility. I was a volunteer firefighter when I lived in Kentucky, and our training captain reminded us regularly about the importance of having a fire-fighter partner when entering a burning structure. Moreover, two fresh firefighters on the outside of the structure served as the Rapid Intervention Team (RIT), ready to rescue any fallen firefighters inside the building. Generally, two firefighters went in together, and two others remained ready to enter as needed. Fighting a fire alone was just too risky.

Spiritual warfare is the same. Fight alone, and you are asking for trouble. Ignore or neglect others in this battle, and you have stepped into the devil's trap. Choose not to walk beside other believers, and the next generation of believers will lose the same battles. When we lean on each other and disciple one another, though, victory is much more often our story. We want that story to be your story—and the story of others you disciple after you've read this book.

A Personal Testimony

I (Chuck) have written elsewhere that I started studying spiritual warfare when Eph 6:12—"our struggle is not against flesh and blood, but against the rulers, against the authorities, against the cosmic powers of this darkness, against evil, spiritual forces in the heavens"—came to life for me.[1] This truth gripped me at a time when I was struggling to love my dad, who at the time was not a believer. He had been a volatile, angry man as we were grow-ing up, and I both feared him and hated him at the same time. My Christian conversion only compounded my guilt over my

---

[1] See Cook and Lawless, *Spiritual Warfare in the Storyline of Scripture*, 324 (see intro., n. 1).

feelings toward him; but, apart from discipleship, I did not know how to overcome these feelings. What Eph 6:12 did was show me that my dad was not my enemy—Satan and his forces were.

Thus, my journey into studying spiritual warfare began with an intensely personal focus. I wanted freedom from my wrong feelings toward my dad. I no longer wanted to face the ongoing conviction and guilt I experienced because I had not overcome these feelings as a believer. When I read books challenging me to recognize particular demons (such as what others identified as demons of hatred or demons of bitterness) that might have been influencing my life, it didn't take long for me to begin looking for demonic forces everywhere. Identifying the demons rather than repenting over my sin became my focus.

I desperately needed someone to correct and teach me along the way, but that had never been my pattern before that point. For example, as a young male who grew up in a home filled with pornography, I regularly faced that temptation alone as a teenager even after I became a believer. In no way was I going to let anyone know my secret. When I later became a pastor, I faced a different struggle of trying to shepherd a people when I had never been discipled myself. I had no one to invest in me and show me "the ropes" of ministry, and I made mistake after mistake. In fact, that God allowed me to stay in ministry at all is only evidence of his grace.

Even later after I married my wife, I had never seen personally how a husband loves his wife as Christ loves the church (Eph 5:21). I selfishly protected my independence and fought my responsibility to give myself fully to become one with my spouse. I loved Pam the best I could, but I just did not know what a godly husband looked like. I was already a pastor then, so I again refrained from asking anyone to guide me. In my personal life, my ministry, and my marriage, I was fighting alone and losing alone far too often. I was neither the disciple nor the disciple maker I should have been.

Much of that changed when I met Robert Coleman, author of the best-selling book *The Master Plan of Evangelism*, when I was a young seminary professor.[2] Dr. Coleman, who for more than sixty years has invested in others, challenged me to spend the rest of my life investing in younger believers. I took that challenge to heart.[3]

It did not take me long, though, to realize I needed someone to mentor me if I were going to mentor others. Though the friendships God has given me differ, older men through the years have modeled Christian faithfulness for me. They have pointed me to Christ by the way they imitate him. I will always be grateful for men such as Sonney, Red, Ed, Ronnie, Mike, Dave, Ralph, and so many others who modeled victory in Christ for me, even when they faced tough times.

These relationships have changed my daily walk with God. They have not only reminded me that I must not face the enemy alone, but they have also shown me God's grace in providing others to walk with me. I have learned that victory is sweetest when others faithfully run the race with us—and even defeat is less consuming when others quickly pick us up and challenge us again. Now I have the privilege of teaching the same to others.

---

[2] Robert Coleman, *Master Plan of Evangelism* (Grand Rapids: Revell, 1993). I tell this story in more detail in Lawless, *Disciple*, 17 (see chap. 7, n. 8).

[3] See Chuck Lawless, *Mentor: How along the Way Discipleship Can Change Your Life* (Nashville: Lifeway, 2018).

That is the prayer that Bill and I pray for you: that God will give you believers who intentionally walk with you and others you might walk beside. We pray you will grow as a victorious disciple of Christ through studying the Scriptures that are the basis for this book. We then pray that other believers will also live in victory because of your witness and example of wearing the full armor of God.

Discipleship and Spiritual Warfare

Matthew's expression of the Great Commission requires us to make disciples of all the peoples of the world (see Matt 28:18–20). That process begins when we *start* encouraging others to be a disciple of Jesus; that is, it starts when we first share the good news of Jesus with someone. That process continues when others follow Christ, we baptize them, and then continually teach them to obey everything Jesus commanded.

The Offensive Nature of Warfare (Again)

Both evangelism and discipleship, in fact, are *offensive spiritual warfare* (though, as we have noted previously, the armor is both offensive and defensive). On one hand, the Bible is clear that nonbelievers follow the "ruler of the power of the air, the spirit now working in the disobedient" (Eph 2:2). They live in the domain of darkness (Col 1:13), are blinded by the god of this age (2 Cor 4:3–4), are caught in the devil's trap (2 Tim 2:26), and operate under the power of Satan (Acts 26:18). These descriptions are numerous and clear: the people God has called us to evangelize are in the devil's kingdom. Thus, we engage the darkness any time we choose to do evangelism.

On the other hand, discipleship is also how we prepare for and fight this battle. If evangelism is engaging the darkness, then discipleship is arming believers for the battle. It is, as we have seen before, teaching others more than just telling them how to follow Christ. We help each other wear the whole armor of God because God calls us to take the gospel of light into the darkness of the enemy's kingdom.

It is no wonder, then, that all the warnings about spiritual warfare in the Bible are addressed to believers. Whether it is Jesus (Matt 6:13), Paul (Eph 6:12), Peter (1 Pet 5:8), James (Jas 4:7), or John (1 John 4:4), their words forewarn believers. We are the target because we are the means God has chosen to proclaim the gospel to the nations. Here is the overall picture built around the armor-of-God passage in Ephesians 6:[4]

1. **Believers cannot defeat the enemy unless we are wearing the full armor of God.** That is just basic Bible (Eph 6:10–17). Believers who threaten the enemy are those who are wearing the armor that is God's in the first place. He who is our warrior grants us power and wisdom to lead others to follow Christ even as enemy forces strike against us. If, on the other hand, we lose the battles because we fight in our own strength, those we are discipling are wounded in the process as well.

---

[4] Chuck Lawless, "A Discipleship Strategy That Takes on the Enemy," Chuck Lawless website, March 4, 2016, https://chucklawless.com /2016/03/6811/.

2. **Wearing the armor is both positional and behavioral.** Perhaps you remember this discussion from chapter 7 in this book. It is both our identity in Christ and our walking in obedience that alarm the enemy. Who we are *and* how we live factor into our preparation for the battles we face. Position without practice can become libertinism (claiming Christian liberty to live however we wish), and practice without position can be legalism. Either one is fertile ground for the enemy.

3. **Believers know how to wear the full armor of God only when we teach them.** Think about new believers. Those baby followers of Christ are likely a threat to Satan simply because they are on fire for God and still know nonbelievers to reach (that is, they are not cocooned in the church world yet). Satan aims his arrows at them through discouragement, doubt, temptation, and any other means he might deem effective. The only way new believers can defend against those attacks is to put on the full armor of God—but how can they do that unless we first teach them about it?

4. **When we do not teach believers how to wear God's armor, they will lose spiritual conflicts.** It happens all the time. That zealous, passionate new believer who once would tell anyone or anything about Jesus somehow loses his fire. His church attendance becomes sporadic, and we wonder what happened to him. Too often, what happened to him is his church did not teach him about spiritual warfare and the armor of God—and he did not know how to fight a battle he did not even

know existed. That is almost inevitable when we do not disciple believers to wear the full armor of God, simply because unarmed warriors do not win battles. At some level, we are responsible for their defeat too.

5. **The longer we wait to invest in new believers, the more likely it is they will be defeated in the conflict.** If we reach new believers but then do not immediately walk with them, we set them up for defeat. In no way does the enemy kindly back off for a while as new believers get grounded in their faith; rather, he who fought to keep them in darkness as nonbelievers immediately attacks them to extinguish their light when they become believers. Any gap between their conversion and our teaching them is an open door for the enemy—and he seldom misses an opening to establish a foothold.

6. **Discipleship should include, in addition to worship and small groups, face-to-face mentoring.** Small-group studies are great—and needed. We have written this book, in fact, in hope that groups will study it together. At the same time, though, believers also need both the corporate experience of congregational worship and face-to-face mentoring (which I understand to be one piece of the discipleship pie) to grow in Christ.[5] Worship turns our attention to God who has already defeated the enemy. Small groups grant us fellowship and teaching to fight the battles together. Mentoring deepens our accountability and gives us a place to discuss our most difficult spiritual battles.

---

[5] See Lawless, *Disciple*, 83–85; Lawless, *Mentor.*

7. **Disciple makers must guard their own lives under attack.** The apostle Paul clearly understood the reality of spiritual warfare (Eph 6:10–20). He knew an evil, sly, scheming power stood against him. What amazes me, though, are Paul's mandates to others even as he faced his own battles: "I urge you to imitate me" (1 Cor 4:16); "Imitate me, as I also imitate Christ" (1 Cor 11:1); "For you yourselves know how you should imitate us" (2 Thess 3:7); "we did it to make ourselves an example to you so that you would imitate us" (2 Thess 3:9).[6] The battle was intensely real for Paul, but still he fought the good fight, ran the race well, and kept the faith (2 Tim 4:6–8). In the end, he could with integrity challenge his protégé Timothy to fulfill his own ministry equally well (2 Tim 4:1–5). That is what good disciple makers do: they wear the full armor of God, fight the fight well, and take seriously their responsibility to live in victory for the sake of others.

8. **This kind of discipleship does not happen by accident.** That is, we must have a strategy to accomplish our goals. The enemy, who is a schemer (Eph 6:11), often wins because he operates with more strategy than our churches do. I have studied North American churches for many years, and my anecdotal evidence suggests that churches think far too little about intentional discipleship. They operate not on strategic planning, but on

---

[6] The writer of Hebrews also called believers to imitate the faith of their leaders: "Remember your leaders who have spoken God's word to you. As you carefully observe the outcome of their lives, imitate their faith" (Heb 13:7).

assumption; they assume that attenders and members who faithfully participate in church activities will almost automatically become fully devoted disciples of Christ.[7] For these churches, activity = discipleship. Perhaps not surprisingly, leaders of these churches often then bear the burden of members who have not truly been discipled. Their congregations remain babies in Christ when they should have already grown, and Satan's forces find them susceptible to their arrows.

9. **No believer ever outgrows the need for someone to walk with him or her.** That is because we do not escape spiritual conflict until the Lord calls us home. In our previous work, in fact, Bill and I added a chapter about "finishing well" because we knew so many long-term believers who had fallen. One of my pastoral mentors, who is in his seventies, has mentors in their eighties and nineties. I learn from all of them even in my sixties, and I get to invest in others much younger than I. I then challenge them to invest in others quickly, and the cycle continues. As long as the battle goes on, teaching one another to wear the full armor of God is not optional.

10. **Discipleship that takes on the enemy can begin in your church today.** If you finish reading this book and walk more in victory without teaching others, you will have missed one of our goals. I will say it again—none of us is to fight these battles alone. Take this challenge, then: begin investing in at least one other believer. Help each other wear the full armor of God and take on the enemy

---

[7] See Lawless, *Disciple*, 10.

for God's glory. Indeed, the rest of this chapter will help you take those steps.

The Role of Mentoring in Discipleship and Warfare [8]

As I write this chapter, I am celebrating the graduation of Kevin, a PhD student I had the privilege of guiding through his doctoral program. I have mentored many doctoral students over the years, but this graduate was special to me because of our long-term friendship. He and I have known each other for more than fifteen years.

I met Kevin when he came to The Southern Baptist Theological Seminary as a student in the Advanced Master of Divinity program. I was the dean of the Billy Graham School of Missions, Evangelism and Church Growth, and he was a student in that school. We connected via not only our interest in theological education, but also our mutual love for hiking and firefighting. In fact, it was Kevin who challenged me when I was forty-eight to fulfill a long-term dream to be a firefighter. He became my assistant at Southern Seminary and later my PhD student at Southeastern Seminary. He counts me as a dad, and his kids know me only as "Papaw Chuck."

I could tell story after story like this one as God has graciously gifted me over the years with men at seminaries and in local churches to disciple and guide. As a mentor, I am privileged to walk beside another believer, investing in him that he might learn more and more about being Christlike. Ideally, my personal relationship with Christ will show him how to imitate Christ.

---

[8] See Lawless, *Mentor*, 74–84.

Both of us then become iron sharpening iron as we walk together (Prov 27:17), provoking each other to good works and challenging each other as needed (Heb 10:23–25).

In my judgment, mentors have at least three responsibilities. First, we teach others to obey what Jesus commanded. Every believer has this mandate from Jesus, so it applies to all of us. Our faith is not only about our following Christ closely, but also about our guiding others to do the same. Indeed, Christians who are not teaching someone to obey Jesus are not fully walking in obedience. The Great Commission (Matt 28:18–20) lets no believer off the hook, and fundamental obedience to Jesus causes the enemy to flee—at least for a while.

Second, mentors must walk closely enough with others while equipping them that the enemy must fight through the mentors to get to the mentees. I picture the mentor walking arm in arm with the mentee, with the mentor carrying the shield of faith while he's also teaching the mentee to walk by faith. The young mentee may be vulnerable as he's learning about the armor of God, but the mentor helps deflect the enemy's arrows while he learns. Together they battle. Together they grow. Together they teach others what they are learning as they seek to make disciples who live in victory. The mentee then becomes a mentor himself, and the cycle of gospel reproduction continues. Nobody fights the battle alone.

Third, mentors pick up mentees who fall and gently restore them (Gal 6:1) if they succumb to the enemy's attacks—and it *does* happen at times. Even the most faithful followers of Christ sometimes experience spiritual defeat that necessitates our prayer and intervention. Timothy George describes this responsibility this way:

While all sin is detestable before God and should be resisted as the plague, certain transgressions are especially hurtful to the fellowship of the church and must be dealt with according to the canons of Christian discipline. Those who are spiritually minded, that is, those whose lives give evidence of the fruit of the Spirit, have a special responsibility to take the initiative in seeking restoration and reconciliation with those who have been caught in such an error.[9]

This commitment to restoration reflects both the pain and the joy of mentoring others amid spiritual warfare. I have discipled some young men who made unwise, sinful choices even after we had begun a discipleship relationship. Some, in fact, necessitated church discipline. In my arrogance, I was certain my influence would keep them on the straight path, but that has not always been the case. I, like many other disciple makers, have shed heavy tears over disciples who, at the time, grieved their sin much less than I did.

Some mentees do fall. They break your heart. They make you weep. If you leave them on the ground, though, the enemy wins. In fact, I have seen the hand of God restoring some of these fallen brothers. God's grace is so great that he holds our hand even when we want to let go. I have watched God overwhelm sinful hearts and bring wayward brothers to brokenness and repentance so they might experience his grace again. Our responsibility as mentors is to walk faithfully with God as we pray and wait, ever watching like the father of the prodigal son

---

[9] George, *Galatians*, 410 (see chap. 3, n. 5).

(Luke 15:11–32) for the return of our sons in the faith—and rejoice with great celebration when they make their way home!

Here I think of Simon Peter, the fisherman turned disciple.[10] His brother Andrew had introduced him to Jesus (John 1:40–42), and they had left their boats on the sea to follow the Lord (Mark 1:16–20). Simon became the leader of the apostles, his name listed first among the disciples in each of the Synoptic Gospels (Matt 10:2; Mark 3:16; Luke 6:14). He is perhaps best known, though, for his choice to deny knowing Jesus when the Lord was arrested.

Jesus warned him about the coming attack: "Simon, Simon, look out. Satan has asked to sift you like wheat" (Luke 22:31). The enemy could not get to Simon without the Lord's permission, but he was nonetheless brazen enough to ask. Jesus's response was surely instructive to Simon and encouraging to us: "But I have prayed for you that your faith may not fail. And you, when you have turned back, strengthen your brothers" (Luke 22:32). The same Jesus who allowed Satan to sift the apostles was the Jesus who would pray Simon Peter through the conflict. Simon would never be alone in the battle.

Satan's attack was strong, striking Simon with fear and enticing him to lie about his relationship with Jesus. With his third denial and the crowing of a rooster, Simon Peter had done exactly what he had just hours before said he would never do (Luke 22:33). He had denied his Lord. It surely seemed at that moment that Satan's victory increased with each successive denial. The rugged fisherman had succumbed to the enemy's arrows, and defeat hung in the air . . . *except* that Luke gives us a detail no other Gospel

[10] See Chuck Lawless, *Nobodies for Jesus* (Franklin, TN: Rainer, 2013), 67–73.

writer included: "Then the Lord turned and looked at Peter" (Luke 22:61). Somehow there is hope written across those words.

Peter had denied knowing the Lord, but the Lord kept his eyes on Peter. He looked at the fleeing fisherman with "eyes full of pain, yet also of pardon,"[11] and the connection of their eyes melted the fisherman. Peter's arrogance became anguish. His confidence became conviction. His toughness became tears; his willpower became weeping.

Still, though, Jesus had already prayed for him—and Jesus would not let Peter fall so far he could not see him. Indeed, Jesus would restore the broken fisherman and use him to proclaim the good news to Jerusalem in Acts 2. The mentor kept the mentee in his sight, and he picked him up when Peter could only weep bitterly in grief and repentance. Even an angel at the empty tomb would only days later graciously make sure Peter knew Jesus was alive (Mark 16:7).

That's what mentors do: pray for their disciples, keep their eyes on them, provoke them to godliness, love them even in their failure, grant them forgiveness as they return, and renew their hope. They walk with their disciples up the mountain and through the valley. The enemy's forces cannot stand long against that kind of sacrificial, discipling love.

Getting Started

How, then, do you get started investing in other believers? Every person is different, so I am hesitant to offer a formulaic, rote method of disciple making. How I invest in one brother is likely

---

[11] William Hendriksen, *Exposition of the Gospel according to Luke*, New Testament Commentary (Grand Rapids: Baker, 1978), 995.

different from how I invest in another. So, start with the person, not with the program. If you start with the program, you will likely treat your mentee as a project more than a Christ-follower who walks with you.

At the same time, though, some basic guidelines might help you get started. Recognizing that I'm giving you only beginning steps, I challenge you to begin somewhere with someone. The devil at least temporarily wins when we do nothing with making disciples.

To begin, pray, and enlist at least one prayer partner to intercede for you as you make this commitment. Don't take a step unless the Lord is leading you (see Exod 33:15–16)—and don't assume you can recognize the Lord's leading apart from prayer. Pray first before you make your plans. Get others to walk the path with you through prayer. If the battle makes it difficult for you to pray, trust the intercessory work of the Son (Heb 7:25; Rom 8:34) and the Spirit (Rom 8:26–27) in those intense moments.

Next, through prayer and in cooperation with believers who know you best, make sure you are wearing the full armor of God. Positionally in Christ and practically in faithfulness, obey the Lord. Turn from sins of commission (that is, in God's power stop ongoing sin in your life) and correct sins of omission (still in God's power, do all that you know God has called believers to do). Make spiritual disciplines part of your DNA. Deal with any hidden sin in your life by confession and repentance. Be sure to walk in truth and righteousness. Be ready in God's strength and might when the enemy comes after you because you choose to disciple others to wear the armor themselves.

Then, prayerfully ask God to help you see someone you might encourage to grow in Christ. Jesus modeled that approach for us as he prayed all night long before calling out his apostles (Luke 6:12). And, perhaps to our surprise, though not to Jesus's, the Father directed him to invest in a group of men who did not always listen, who sometimes failed in ministry, and who often argued about who was the greatest. One betrayed him, another denied him, and all fled when Jesus was arrested. They were, as I have often described them, "knuckleheads" at times—but they were part of the Father's plan. You and I, by the way, are knuckleheads sometimes, too, but God specializes in knuckleheads!

As you are praying, keep checking until you find someone who wants to grow in Christ, and spend some time together. You might note that I've not given much direction here—except to say, don't give up if the first persons you ask aren't interested or available. In fact, I encourage you not to get too hung up on a strategy when you begin a mentoring relationship. Some disciple-making relationships are more formal, with regularly scheduled meetings and set curriculum. Others are quite informal, with one-on-one life conversations in various settings. The goal in either case includes instruction, but disciple makers need be only one step ahead of others to teach them something about walking with God.

The enemy may try to convince you that you are either (1) too untrained to offer anything to anyone or (2) too significant to lower yourself to help others. Do not listen to either voice; just walk with God and trust him to show you the way. Do push each other to love the Lord and do good works that honor him, but you might do that over a biweekly meal, a fishing trip, a shopping spree, a leisurely walk, or some other activity that allows you to spend time together and talk. Availability + conversation in the context of a God-centered relationship makes good mentoring.

You will likely find that the conversations in these relationships move in multiple directions. Many will revolve around our spiritual walk. Some will tackle theological issues. In other cases, though, the conversation might address topics like marriage, parenting, vocation, budgeting, housing, automobiles, gardening, and anything else mentees might be wondering about. That is still discipleship as long as we're helping each other become more Christlike, think more Christianly, and follow God more completely in all areas of our lives.

On the other hand, a mentoring relationship that focuses on head knowledge alone is not fully discipleship; it is a tutoring session. So, do not just talk about something or study something in the mentoring relationship. Instead, *do something*, building on your study that shows obedience to God and ministers to others. Pray together. Visit a church member in the hospital. Do evangelism. Minister to widows and orphans. Take a mission trip together. Secure clearance to visit inmates in a local prison. Do community outreach. Teach vacation Bible school. Do something, recognizing that discipleship that stays in the head and never translates to the feet does not alarm the enemy.

Finally, be the person you need to be as you model faith in front of others: a consistent man or woman of God. I work most often with young people, and I can say with certainty they show little interest in structured meetings, superficial discussions, inconsistent commitments, shallow vulnerability, or cultural Christianity.[12] What they long to see is Christian authenticity—

---

[12] Chuck Lawless, "Mentoring That Usually Won't Work with Christian Millennials," Chuck Lawless website, April 9, 2019, https://chucklawless.com/2019/04/mentoring-that-usually-wont-work-with-christian-millennials/

a "death to self" genuine faith they have seldom seen in other adults. They know believers whose faith is real to some extent, but they do not always know many whose trust is deep and whose commitment is undying. These young folks want to make an eternal difference; they recognize, however, that lukewarm believers "will not be God's force set apart to make a dent in the darkness of the world."[13] You and I have opportunity to be, and to help them be, the kind of force that drives back the darkness.

Indeed, I close this chapter with a question: Are you so faithfully a reproducing follower of Christ that the enemy strikes at you? This battle is real for God's people as we face principalities and powers (Eph 6:12). It is possible, though, that you seemingly do not face much spiritual attack—and even reading this book has not heated up the conflict. Think about why that might be the case, and do a self-evaluation of your own life as we press toward the end of this study.[14]

It might be, for example, that you are in a God-given season of rest. Sometimes we find ourselves under a less serious time of spiritual attack, and that time almost feels like a break—a blessing of God that allows us to focus on him, all the while knowing that the enemy will come back at a more "opportune time" (Luke 4:13 ESV). Those seasons are usually brief, and they do not happen often for the believer who genuinely wants to seek and honor God.

As difficult as it is for me to put into writing, it might also be that you are not a genuine believer. As we noted earlier in

[13] Lawless, *Nobodies for Jesus*, 2.

[14] Chuck Lawless, "3 Reasons You May Not Be under Spiritual Attack," Chuck Lawless website, October 18, 2017, https://chucklawless.com/2017/10/3-reasons-you-may-not-be-under-spiritual-attack/.

this chapter, nonbelievers are in the enemy's kingdom. And those who are already in his camp do not frighten him. If you are not certain of your relationship with God, review the gospel story below and turn to Christ. Tell somebody else the decision you have made—and be a trophy of God's grace.

The Gospel in a Nutshell

- God created all of us in his image (Gen 1:26–27), and we are all accountable to him (Rev 4:11).
- We have all chosen to rebel against him (Isa 53:6); that is, all of us have sinned (Rom 3:23).
- The penalty for our rebellion is death (Rom 6:23), but God offers us the gift of eternal life through the death of his Son, Jesus, who bore God's wrath on the cross and then broke the power of death through resurrection (Matt 28:1–10; Rom 5:8; 1 Pet 2:24–25; 3:18; 1 John 4:10).
- If we confess our sins and turn away from them—that is, repent—and trust Jesus to save us, he will forgive us for our rebellion and give us new and eternal life (Mark 1:15; Acts 16:30–31; Rom 5:1–2; 10:9–10). Simply praying a prayer cannot save you, but we do encourage you to talk to God as you follow his command to repent and believe.

On the other hand, you might be a genuine believer—but one who is hardly a threat to the enemy. Satan and his forces are not much concerned about believers who continually give in to temptation and ignore the command to make disciples through evangelism and equipping. He is not alarmed when we go through the motions of church in our own power. He does not get stressed when we live so close to the world that nonbelievers see no transforming power in the gospel. Though the story of Acts 19:11–15 is not exactly what I am describing here, too many believers today live in such a way that the enemy says, "Jesus I know. Paul I know. But who are you?" He wastes few arrows on people who are not even on his radar.

So, does this mean that we should welcome spiritual warfare? Not at all. It simply means that we live in the tension of crying out, "Father . . . deliver us from the evil one" (Matt 6:9–13) even as we invade the enemy's darkness with the light of the gospel. Press on, wearing the full armor of God!

Conclusion

I have the privilege of walking alongside young men at the seminary where I teach and in the local church where I serve. Even this week, I have had lunches with two brothers I have grown to love and respect as we walk the Christian journey together. I also have in my office pictures of several others I have invested in over the years. These brothers are now serving all around the world. The pictures are now dated, but they bring back great memories for me.

One of my favorite books is Michael Card's *The Walk*, a story of a mentoring relationship between Michael and one of his professors, Dr. Bill Lane. Dr. Lane was known for his pithy statements that packed great wisdom into short, memorable statements. One of those statements I have never forgotten after reading this book decades ago is "When God gives a gift, he wraps it in a person."[15]

---

[15] Michael Card, *The Walk* (Nashville: Thomas Nelson, 2000), 4.

That primary gift was Jesus, but God also wraps his gifts to us in others. We get to influence them, but my experience is that they influence us just as much. When others are paying attention to your life, you will likely pay more attention to it, too. When they are looking for godly examples, you will want to be one. When they look to you for guidance, you will want the Lord's wisdom.

And, when they face the reality of three enemies—the world, the flesh, and the devil—coming after them, you will want to be in the trenches with them. You will want to live in victory yourself and then model for them how to do the same, each of you pushing the other to submit to God and resist the devil. Victory over the enemy is especially sweet when we can celebrate together with others who know God is their warrior.

CONCLUSION

Where Do We Go from Here?

You have made it to the final chapter of this book, and Bill and I are grateful you have joined us for this study. Our prayer along the way as we have written this book is that readers would find true victory over the enemy by focusing on Christ— and we pray that has happened for you.

Taking Next Steps

A word of caution and challenge is in order here, however. Now that you have almost completed this book, the enemy will likely do what he can to snatch from you any teaching or idea you have found helpful, encouraging, or convicting. He does that to nonbelievers when they hear the gospel (Mark 4:14–15), but he also hammers at believers likewise when we want to grow in the Word. Meanwhile, the power of the world will pull at your soul, and your flesh will fight against what you know you need to do.

Sometimes those attacks are blatant. Temptation increases. Doubt grows. Fear develops. People frustrate us. Bible reading is tedious. Prayer is hard. Isolation occurs as we pull away from other believers. Under the weight of an intense battle, you wonder if it was worth reading a book on spiritual warfare.

In other cases, the attack is less obvious—more a distraction than a direct hit. Life goes on, and you have other family and work responsibilities to capture your time. Even your commitment to service through your local church can become consuming at times. The excitement of studying a book on spiritual warfare dies down as you move further and further from the study. You do not intend to ignore what you have learned, but still you find yourself neglecting (and sometimes even forgetting) what you've read here.

Either way, the battle is on. The schemer is at work.

So, what should you do? Or, more appropriately in this book, what should *we* do? Start by taking one step of obedience toward Christ. Decide one thing you can do today that will turn your attention to God and weaken the enemy's strategy at the same time. Even as I write this conclusion, I am thinking of steps I, too, need to take in the right direction.

Maybe the first step for you is to secure some prayer partners who will intercede for you regularly. I can tell you from experience that fighting spiritual battles is easier when you know that somebody you trust has been praying for you. One of my mentors prays for me every morning—and I often think of that gift when the days get difficult. Someone who knows how to walk in victory over the enemy is touching heaven daily on my behalf. That is a blessing you cannot quantify.

Another step might be to use your ten-minute segments as we have suggested in this book. Even ten minutes with the Lord each day in prayer and Bible study can contribute to your spiritual growth, and you will eventually see those ten minutes expand as you grow in your love for the Lord. Take a drink of the Lord's goodness, and you will thirst for more. In fact, you might so long for him that fasting becomes a regular part of your life.

Another option might be to talk with a trusted believer about an area where the enemy seems to be winning in your life. Whatever that area might be, keeping it in the darkness is not a step toward victory. Appropriately confess your struggle to someone and make intentional plans for accountability. Invite someone else to help you wear the full armor of God.

One move in this direction might be to start doing Scripture memorization more regularly. As I write this final chapter, I have just today talked with a pastor friend about a potential health issue for someone I love. I needed him to pray for me (which he did), but he asked me a question I had not expected: "What Scripture verses have you memorized that can give you strength in a time of waiting and worry like this?" I had answers, though I'm certain my verses didn't fall off my lips immediately like his verses do for him. You, like I, might need to take a first step to strengthen this part of your spiritual disciplines (and maybe you can start with one of the verses at the end of this chapter).

Consider also getting more invested in your local church if you are not already. God's people are hardly perfect, and they may really stress you out sometimes—but they are still the family of God. We weaken the enemy's hold when we thank God for messy people and still love them in their messiness, as the apostle Paul showed us in 1 Cor 1:4–9 and 16:24. Hardly was there a more messed up church in the New Testament, but he loved them anyway. You need God's people in your life, and they need you. So, invest with them. Serve alongside them. Pray for them. Win the battles together.

You might even need to seek someone's forgiveness as you work to build relationships in the body of Christ. The enemy knows that unforgiveness hinders our praying (Matt 6:14–15; Mark 11:25), so I suspect he delights when we idolize our pain and refuse to let go of our bitterness. Our hearts then remain in turmoil. Our peace disappears, and our joy diminishes. Believers and nonbelievers alike then begin to question the power of our faith—and the world, the flesh, and the devil seem to have the upper hand temporarily. Do not let that happen in your life; take a step toward forgiveness today.

This next possible first step might catch you off guard, but it is an important one. Bill and I believe strongly that it is our responsibility as church leaders to "call out the called," that is, to challenge Christ-followers to give their lives to ministry. We cannot know the situation of all our readers, but I suspect some of you sense a call to ministry you have not yet publicly accepted. You know the Lord wants you to do something, whether it be full-time or bi-vocational, pastor or missionary, a role you recognize or one you have not yet considered. The enemy will want you to ignore that calling ("You don't really want to do that, do you? Look what it will cost you," he says), but we are challenging you to stand firmly against him through your obedience. In cooperation with your church leaders, deflect the enemy's arrows with the shield of faith. We can tell you from experience that ministry, even with all its challenges, is incredibly exciting.

Finally, you might review the teachings of this book as your first step toward victory over the enemy. Years ago, I wrote a blog post titled "14 Verses for the Spiritual Battle."[1] I have included it here so you might review these victorious truths right now:

1. **Genesis 3:14–15** *Then the Lord God said to the serpent: . . . ["]I will put hostility between you and the woman, and between your seed and her seed. He will strike your head, and you will strike his heel.*

   It was God Himself who put the enmity—the hostility—between the seed of the serpent and the seed of the woman; thus, He must have a purpose for the battle.

2. **Exodus 15:3** *The Lord is a warrior; Yahweh is His name."*

   It's really quite simple: God is our warrior. And He does not lose. Period.

3. **1 Samuel 17:47** *. . . and this whole assembly will know that it is not by sword or by spear that the Lord saves, for the battle is the Lord's. He will hand you over to us.*

   David got it right. The battle is God's, and he delivers according to his own plans.

4. **2 Kings 6:16** *Elisha said, "Don't be afraid, for those who are with us outnumber those who are with them."*

   God's forces may be unseen, but they are not unaware or unavailable. The size of the enemy's forces need not worry us.

---

[1] Chuck Lawless, "14 Verses for the Spiritual Battle," Chuck Lawless website, April 2021, https://chucklawless.com/2021/04/14-verses-for-the -spiritual-battle/.

5. **2 Chronicles 20:15** *This is what the Lord says: "Do not be afraid or discouraged because of this vast number, for the battle is not yours, but God's."*

   Jahaziel spoke truth. If the battle is the Lord's, we do not need to be afraid or discouraged.

6. **Job 1:9[–10]** *Satan answered the Lord, "Does Job fear God for nothing? Haven't You placed a hedge around him, his household, and everything he owns?"*

   Even when God gives the enemy permission to attack us, Satan knows he cannot go beyond God's protection. The Enemy knows about God's hedges.

7. **Matthew 4:10–11** *Then Jesus told him, "Go away, Satan! For it is written: Worship the Lord your God, and serve only Him." Then the Devil left him.*

   That's the way it works: Jesus says, "Get away," and the devil flees. He has to.

8. **Mark 1:23[–24]** *Just then a man with an unclean spirit was in their synagogue. He cried out, "What do you have to do with us, Jesus—Nazarene? Have you come to destroy us? I know who you are—the Holy One of God!"*

   The demons know who Jesus is. He's the Holy One who has come to destroy them.

9. **Luke 22:31–32** *"Simon, Simon, look out! Satan has asked to sift you like wheat. But I have prayed for you that your faith may not fail."*

   Not only must Satan get permission to sift us, but the same Jesus who gives him permission to attack us is the One who prays us through the conflict. He never leaves us alone.

10. **Romans 16:20** *The God of peace will soon crush Satan under your feet.*

    The God who gives us peace is also the God who defeats the Enemy in the battle. God will keep his word of Genesis 3:15—Satan will not win.

11. **2 Corinthians 12:7–10** *Therefore, so that I would not exalt myself, a thorn in the flesh was given to me, a messenger of Satan to torment me. . . . For when I am weak, then I am strong.*

    The Enemy's attacks may weaken us, but in God's plan we defeat him by our weakness—not by our strength. "God, make me weak" is, in God's economy, a prayer for victory.

12. **Ephesians 6:10–11** *Finally, be strengthened by the Lord and by his vast strength. Put on the full armor of God.*

    [This entire volume has pushed us in this direction.] The strength we do have is God's strength. The armor we wear is God's armor. Victory in warfare is never about us—and that's a good thing.

13. **1 John 4:4** *. . . the one who is in you is greater than the one who is in the world.*

    God lives in us. That's amazing. That's also our guarantee of victory.

14. **Revelation 12:11** *They conquered him by the blood of the Lamb and by the word of their testimony, for they did not love their lives in the face of death.*

    Even if we die in the battle, we still win.

    When we get that truth right, the enemy can't hurt us anymore.

Keeping Our Focus Right

We cannot close this book without taking us again to the center of the story: God. Bill and I don't know what battles you might be facing today or will face tomorrow, but we want to turn our attention to God as we pray for you. Hear our pastoral prayer, and let it give you hope today:

> Father, we have victory because of you. You give us strength. You give us armor. You give us peace. We thank you for the privilege of expressing these truths through writing this book. Take it, and use it for your glory in our lives and in the lives of our readers. Where the struggle is real, give victory even in weakness. Where some are lingering too close to the sin line, send your angels to rescue them. Where some are even now making plans for first steps toward victory, give them other believers to walk with them. Allow them to see glimpses of victory in you.
>
> And, Lord, call us out in your power to take the gospel to our neighbors and the nations. Free others from darkness as we do your work together. May the devil be dislodged all around the world through the faithful efforts of believers wearing your armor. We will look forward, God, to the day when we will all live in victory eternally. In the meantime, give us victory today.
>
> All these things we ask in the name of Jesus, the risen and conquering Savior. Amen.

Amen, indeed. In him we have victory over the enemy.

Subject Index

Scripture Index